Presenting Boston...
A COOKBOOK
By The Junior League of Boston, Inc.

On The Cover

Reproduction of an engraving by Carwitham enti͏̈   ͏̈outh
East View of the Great Town of Boston in New͏̈   ͏̈ngland in
America," printed in London. Scene is in 1743.

Courtesy of the Bostonian Society
Old State House, Boston, Massachusetts

The Junior League of Boston, Inc.
Boston, Massachusetts

First Printing 5,000 — April 1976
Second Printing 5,000 — January 1977
Third Printing 5,000 — July 1977
Fourth Printing 5,000 — January 1978
Fifth Printing 5,000 — October 1979
Sixth Printing 5,000 — January 1980
Seventh Printing 10,000 — July 1981
Eighth Printing 10,000 — January 1984

For additional copies use order blank in back of the book or write directly to:

PRESENTING BOSTON
The Junior League of Boston, Inc.
117 Newbury St.
Boston, Massachusetts 02116

Checks should be made payable in the amount of $10.95 each plus $1.50 postage and handling each.

Massachusetts residents add 55¢ sales tax per book.

Printed in the United States of America
ISBN 0-9604156-0-2
Library of Congress Catalog Card Number A753882

KANSAS CITY
PRESS, INC.

THE COOKBOOK PEOPLE

Olathe, Kansas
800/821-5745

Foreword

HE RECIPES in PRESENTING BOSTON are as varied as the geographic origins of the women who contributed them. Because of Boston's historical importance as a center of trade and culture, the city has long been a magnet for people from all over the world. These recipes reflect this diversity.

To give you some idea of the events that influenced Boston since its earliest days, we have included a variety of early prints. We are grateful to the Bostonian Society, the Mariners Museum, Newport News, Virginia, the Massachusetts Historical Society, and the Museum of Fine Arts for their generosity in making them available.

The recipes were contributed by the members of the Junior League of Boston. Each recipe has been thoroughly tested and enthusiastically accepted by a team of testers to whom we are most grateful.

The purpose of the Junior League of Boston, Inc. "is exclusively educational and charitable and is to promote voluntarism, to develop the potential of its members for voluntary participation in community affairs and to demonstrate the effectiveness of trained volunteers."

The proceeds from the sale of the cookbook will be returned to the community through the Community Program Trust.

Table of Contents

Hors d'oeuvres

Artichoke Squares

Comments: Quiche-like!

Preparation time: 20 minutes   Cooking time: 30 minutes

2 6-oz. jars marinated
   artichoke hearts
1 small onion, finely chopped
1 clove garlic, mashed
4 eggs
1/4 cup dry bread crumbs

1/4 tsp. salt
1/8 tsp. pepper
1/8 tsp. oregano
1/8 tsp. Tabasco
1/2 lb. Cheddar cheese,
   shredded
2 tbsp. parsley, minced

Drain the juice from one jar of artichoke hearts into a frying pan. Discard juice from the second jar. Chop artichokes; set aside. Saute the onion and garlic in the artichoke liquid until the onion is transparent. Beat eggs in a small bowl until frothy; add bread crumbs, salt, pepper, oregano and Tabasco. Stir in the cheese, parsley, chopped artichokes and onion mixture. Turn into a buttered 7 x 11 inch baking pan and bake for 30 minutes at 325°. Let cool in the pan, then cut into 1″ squares. Serve cold or reheat at 325° for 10-12 minutes.

Smoked Beef Dip

Comments: Terrific in quantity for a large party.

Preparation time: 7-8 minutes   Cooking time: 15 minutes

**1 pkg. smoked beef,
chopped**
**8 oz. cream cheese,
softened**
1/2 cup soured cream
1-1/2 tbsp. onion, minced

**1-1/2 tbsp. green peppers,
minced**
1-1/2 tbsp. celery, minced
1 tbsp. milk
**1-1/2 tbsp. walnuts,
crushed**

Combine cream cheese, milk and soured cream. Blend in remaining ingredients except walnuts, and mix until thoroughly combined. Pour into a small baking dish and sprinkle the top with the walnuts. Bake at 350° for 15-20 minutes. Serve hot with crackers or chips.

Camembert Butter

Comments: A delicately flavoured mixture.

Preparation time: 10 minutes

Combine equal amounts of Camembert and sweet butter. Season with grated onion and paprika to taste. Serve on small thin slices of dark rye bread.

Caviar Mousse Cordon Bleu

Comments: A lovely way to stretch caviar!

Preparation time: 30 minutes   Cooking time: 5 minutes

1 envelope unflavoured gelatin
1/4 cup water
1/2 cup hot white wine
3-1/2 oz. jar black caviar
4 hard-boiled eggs, grated

1/2 cup home-made
  mayonnaise*
1 tbsp. onion, grated
dash Worcestershire sauce
salt to taste

If home-made mayonnaise is not available, a combination of commercial mayonnaise and soured cream may be substituted.

Dissolve the gelatin in water, then stir in the hot wine. Place the caviar in a sieve and rinse thoroughly with cold water. Gently blend the caviar and remaining ingredients into the gelatin mixture. Pour into a lightly oiled mold and chill several hours. Unmold onto a chilled platter; garnish with sprigs of fresh parsley.

Note: Lumpfish or Beluga equally acceptable.

Caviar Mousse Rouge

Comments: Colorful — perfect at Holiday time.

Preparation time: 15-20 minutes   Cooking time: 5 minutes

6 oz. red caviar
1/4 cup parsley, chopped
1 tbsp. onion, grated
1 tsp. lemon rind, grated
1 pint soured cream

1 cup heavy cream, whipped
1 envelope unflavoured gelatin
1/4 cup water
freshly ground pepper

Combine caviar, parsley, onion and lemon rind in a large bowl. Stir in soured cream and set aside. Sprinkle gelatin over water in a saucepan and cook, stirring constantly, over low heat until the gelatin is completely dissolved. Stir gelatin into caviar and soured cream mixture. Fold in whipped cream and add freshly ground pepper to taste. Spoon into a lightly oiled mold and chill until set. Unmold onto lettuce and serve with thin squares of pumpernickel bread spread with sweet butter.

Note: For first course, use 8 individual molds.

Russian Delight

Comments: Inexpensive, but with "a touch of class."

Preparation time: 5 minutes

8 oz. cream cheese	1/2 fresh lemon
onion salt	hard boiled egg
2 oz. black caviar (lumpfish)	chives or parsley

Unwrap and flatten block of cheese slightly; sprinkle with onion salt. Spread caviar over the top and squeeze lemon over all. Refrigerate for at least 30 minutes and garnish with grated hard-boiled egg, chives or parsley. Serve with melba toast.

View of State Street in 1801 after Marston's Painting
Courtesy of the Bostonian Society, Old State House, Boston, Massachusetts

Hors d'oeuvres

Caviar Pie

Comments: Simple and elegant.

Preparation time: 30 minutes

2 oz. black caviar
2 hard-boiled eggs
2 tbsp. mayonnaise

Sieve hard boiled eggs and bind together with 2 tbsp. of mayonnaise. Oil a 4″ flan mold with olive or vegetable oil. Press egg into mold and chill until firm. Spread the caviar into the mold; chill. Unmold onto a chilled plate, garnish, and serve with party rye or crisp toast rounds.

Clam Puffs with Bacon

YIELD: 3 DOZ.

Comments: A touch of the sea practically ready on your pantry shelf or in your freezer.

Preparation time: 15-20 minutes   Cooking time: 25 minutes

1-1/2 cups seasoned dry stuffing mix   1 tsp. lemon juice
8-oz. can minced clams   1 lb. bacon

Mix the lemon juice and clams including liquid in a large bowl. Add the stuffing and mix with a fork until uniformly moist. Cut each strip of bacon into 2 pieces. Divide the clam mixture into 1″ balls, wrap each with a piece of bacon and secure with a toothpick. Place on a broiler pan and bake at 350° for 25 minutes, or until the bacon is cooked. These may be made 24 hours in advance and refrigerated.

Note: If the puffs are frozen, adjust cooking time accordingly. They will require an extra 5-10 minutes.

Crab Florentine

Comments: Marvelous!

Preparation time: 25 minutes   Cooking time: 10 minutes

2 bunches scallions, diced	2 pkgs. frozen chopped
2 cloves garlic, mashed	spinach, cooked and drained
1/4 lb. butter, melted	7 oz.-can crabmeat
1 drop Tabasco	3 oz. Parmesan cheese, grated

Mix scallions, garlic and spinach in melted butter. Add crabmeat and cheese. Season to taste with salt and pepper and a dash of Tabasco. Keep warm in a chafing dish. Serve with pumpernickel.

Hors d'oeuvres   15

Crab Mousse

Comments: Especially nice in hot weather.

Preparation time: 15 minutes

1/4 cup cold water	6 oz. crabmeat, drained,
1 tsp. unflavoured gelatin	shredded
1 lb. cream cheese, softened	dash ground pepper
1/2 tsp. salt	1/4 cup parsley, chopped
2 tbsp. dry sherry	parsley sprigs for garnish

Sprinkle gelatin over water to soften, then stir over low heat until the gelatin is completely dissolved. Beat in cream cheese until smooth. Stir in remaining ingredients and pour into an oiled 3-cup mold. Refrigerate 4 hours or until set. Turn out onto chilled platter and garnish with sprigs of parsley.

Hors d'oeuvres

Crabmeat Coonamessett

Comments: A Cape favorite!

Preparation time: 20-30 minutes
(allow for overnight refrigeration)

12 oz. cream cheese, softened	1 small onion, grated
2 tbsp. Worcestershire sauce	dash garlic salt
1 tbsp. lemon juice	6 oz. chili sauce
2 tbsp. mayonnaise	7 oz. crabmeat, shredded
	3 tbs. fresh parsley, chopped

Combine cream cheese, Worcestershire sauce, lemon juice, mayonnaise, onion and garlic salt. Spread this mixture in a shallow serving dish. Spread chili sauce over the cheese then top with crab. Refrigerate overnight. Garnish with parsley just before serving.

Crabmeat Profiteroles

SERVES 6-8

Comments: Something very special!

Preparation time: 30 minutes   Cooking time: 25 minutes

8 oz. cream cheese, softened
1 tbsp. milk
1/2 tsp. horseradish
1/4 tsp. salt
dash pepper
7 oz. crabmeat

2 tbsp. onion, chopped
1/2 cup boiling water
1/4 cup butter
2 eggs
1/2 cup flour
1/3 cup almonds, finely chopped

Combine softened cream cheese with milk, horseradish, salt and pepper and mix until smooth. Fold in crabmeat, onion and almonds. Set aside. Combine water and butter in a saucepan and stir over medium heat until butter has melted. Add the flour all at once and stir until the dough forms a ball. Remove from heat and let stand for 5 minutes; then add eggs, one at a time. Beat dough until it is stiff. If the dough is not stiff, set aside for 10 minutes, then try again. Place 1/2 teaspoon of dough for each profiterole on a buttered baking sheet and bake at 350° for 10 minutes. Cool, split, and fill with crabmeat mixture. Bake at 350° for 10 minutes.

Note: If made in advance, reheat at 325° for 5-10 minutes.

Domino Bread

Comments: A beautiful checkerboard effect — fantastically good.

Preparation time: 30 minutes

3 narrow loaves French bread
1 lb. Swiss cheese, diced
1 lb. Genoa salami, diced
1 lb. Polish ham, diced
2 hard-boiled eggs, diced

2 large (4") Polish pickles, diced
3/4 cup butter, softened
1 tube anchovy paste

Cream butter and anchovy paste. Remove the ends from the bread and cut each loaf into three sections. Remove the "pulp" from the center of each section of bread with handle of a wooden spoon leaving the crust "tube" intact. Combine anchovy butter with all other ingredients, and stuff each bread tube with the mixture. Be gentle, taking care to fill each section to the center, but not overstuffing them. If they bulge, the crust will burst. Wrap the sections in damp linen kitchen towels and refrigerate until serving time. Just before serving, cut each section into slices less than 1/2" thick and arrange on a serving platter.

Marinated Eggplant

Comments: Poor man's caviar!

Preparation time: 15 minutes
(allow for 5 hours' refrigeration)

Cooking time: 1 hour

2 lbs. eggplant	1 tbsp. cider vinegar
1/2 cup onions, chopped	1/4 cup olive oil
1 cup fresh tomatoes, peeled and chopped	1/2 tsp. freshly ground pepper
	1-1/2 tsp. salt
1 slice white bread, crust removed and crumbled	1/2 tsp. sugar

Wrap eggplant in foil and bake for 1 hour at 375°, opening foil for the last 15 minutes of baking. Cool. Peel and chop eggplant and combine with the onions, tomatoes and bread. Blend the rest of the ingredients together and add to the eggplant mixture. Chill for at least 5 hours, stirring occasionally. Serve on thin pumpernickel bread.

Note: 1-1/2 cup of chopped black olives may be added to the eggplant mixture.

Easy Escargots

Comments: So much simpler than the snail's own shell.

Preparation time: 5 minutes   Cooking time: 5-6 minutes

4 tbsp. butter, softened
1 clove garlic, minced
24 large fresh mushroom
   caps

24 snails, rinsed
   and drained
4 tsp. Parmesan cheese, grated
2 tbsp. fresh parsley, chopped

Combine the butter and minced garlic. Spread half of this mixture in the bottom of a shallow baking dish, and dot the mushroom caps with the remaining portion. Arrange the mushrooms in a single layer in the baking dish, topping each one with a snail. Sprinkle with Parmesan cheese and parsley and broil 5-7 inches away from heat source for 5-6 minutes or until heated through. Serve immediately.

Note: Serves 4 to 6 as a first course.

Escargots Provencale

Comments: Country-style snails. Marvelous for a
first course, too!

Preparation time: 20 minutes   Cooking time: 20 minutes

24 large snails	1 cup onions, minced
1/2 cup dry white wine	4 tsp. garlic, minced
4 tomatoes, cut in wedges	4 1″-thick slices of
or 15 oz. can, drained	French bread, toasted
8 tbsp. butter	

Cook snails in white wine over moderate heat for 10 minutes;
drain. At the same time, simmer the tomatoes in 6 tbsp. of
butter for 10 minutes; add half of the minced onions and 3 tsp.
of the garlic and simmer for an additional 3 minutes. Melt
remaining butter, add snails and cook briskly for 3 minutes
stirring constantly; add the remaining onion and garlic and
cook 1 minute. Arrange French bread on four warmed plates;
spoon half of the tomato sauce over the bread; place 6 snails
on each slice of bread and cover with the remaining tomato
sauce. Serve immediately.

Glazed Meatballs

Comments: A sweet and sour version.

Preparation time: 25 minutes   Cooking time: 15 minutes

1-1/2 lbs. lean ground beef	1-1/3 tsp. flour
1 tsp. Accent	3 tbsp. butter
1 tsp. salt	1/3 cup unsulphured molasses
1/2 small onion, chopped	1/3 cup ketchup
3/4 cup bread crumbs	1/4 tsp. oregano
1/3 cup milk	

Mix ground beef, Accent, salt, onion, bread and milk together. Form into walnut-size meatballs; set aside. Melt butter in a frying pan, stir in flour; when smooth, add molasses, ketchup and oregano. Boil sauce for several minutes, then add meatballs and cook an additional 15 minutes, turning meatballs occasionally to glaze them. Remove sauce and meatballs to chafing dish.

Note: A delicious main course over rice.

Marinated Mushrooms I

Comments: Two versions of a piquant h'ors d'oeuvre or relish.

Preparation time: 20 minutes   Cooking time: 20 minutes
(allow for overnight refrigeration)

1 lb. fresh mushrooms	1/4 tsp. oregano
4 tbsp. olive oil	1 bay leaf
1 tbsp. lemon juice	1 cup tomatoes, peeled, chopped
1 garlic clove, minced	and drained
1 large onion, sliced	1/3 cup wine vinegar
1/4 tsp. thyme	dash sugar
1/4 tsp. marjoram	salt, pepper and Tabasco to taste

Saute the mushrooms in 2 tbsp. of the olive oil. When golden, transfer the mushrooms to a bowl and toss with lemon juice. Saute the onions and garlic in the remaining olive oil. Add seasonings, tomatoes, vinegar, sugar, salt, pepper and Tabasco. Add a little juice from the tomatoes if canned are used. Bring to a boil and simmer 15 minutes. Add marinade to mushrooms, cover tightly and refrigerate overnight.

Note: Keeps well in the refrigerator for a week or longer.

Marinated Mushrooms II

YIELD: 1-1/2-2 CUPS

Preparation time: 15 minutes
(allow for overnight refrigeration)

Cooking time: 5 minutes

1/2 cup wine vinegar
1/2-2/3 cup olive oil
1 tsp. oregano
1 clove garlic, minced
1/2 tsp. salt
1/2 tsp. pepper

1/2 tsp. brown sugar
1 tbsp. lemon juice
1 tsp. prepared mustard
2 tsp. dried parsley flakes
1 small onion, finely sliced
1 lb. fresh mushrooms,
    sliced thickly

Combine all ingredients except mushrooms in a saucepan and bring to a boil. Remove marinade from heat and cool. Add mushrooms to the cooled marinade and refrigerate in a tightly covered bowl overnight. Remove mushrooms from marinade with a slotted spoon just before serving.

Note: These marinated mushrooms can also be used sparingly with the marinade as a salad dressing over romaine.

Martha's Muffins

SERVES 8-10

Comments: An adaption of a Vineyard specialty.

Preparation time: 15 minutes   Cooking time: 15 minutes

1 pkg. English muffins, split
8 oz. American cheese, grated
1/2 cup ripe olives, chopped
1/4 cup scallions, chopped

2 tsp. curry powder
1/2 cup mayonnaise
softened butter

Lightly butter the English muffins. Combine the cheese, olives, scallions, curry powder and mayonnaise. Spread the mixture on the muffins and cut each muffin into quarters. Bake at 350° for 10-15 minutes, or until they are lightly browned and bubbly.

Note: Mixture (without muffins) keeps well in refrigerator for several days.

Boston Common
from The Boston Miscellany, 1842
Courtesy of the Bostonian Society, Old State House, Boston, Massachusetts

Hors d'oeuvres

Pate Maison

Comments: A taste of Britanny

Preparation time: 1 hour   Cooking time: 15 minutes
(allow for overnight refrigeration)

1/2 lb. butter	1/4 cup brandy
1 lb. chicken livers	3 tbsp. heavy cream
1/2 cup onions, chopped	1 tbsp. lemon juice
2 tbsp. shallots, chopped	1 tsp. salt
1/4 cup tart apple, chopped	1/4 tsp. pepper

Place 10 tbsp. of the butter in a bowl and set aside to soften.
Wash, dry and cut livers in half. Saute onion in 3 tbsp. of
butter for 5 minutes; add shallots and apples and cook gently
until apple is tender; remove to blender. Saute chicken livers in
the same skillet, using the remaining 3 tbsp. of butter. Cook for
4 minutes, add brandy and cook for an additional 2 minutes.
Place chicken livers in blender with other ingredients. Add the
cream and blend until smooth. Cool in blender; add the 10 tbsp.
of softened butter and blend on high until pate is thoroughly
mixed. Add lemon, salt and pepper to taste. Pour into a lightly
oiled mold, cover tightly and refrigerate overnight. Unmold
and garnish.

Note: Filled mold may be sealed with clarified butter.

Reubenettes

Comments: Let guests prepare their own versions of this popular Deli treat.

Prepare a platter of thinly sliced corned beef, thinly sliced Swiss cheese, cold sauerkraut, and "party loaf" slices of rye bread. Serve with bowls of Dijon mustard and horseradish.

Note: Prepared open face sandwiches can be placed under broiler until cheese is bubbly.

Sausage Slices

Comments: Quick and delicious!

Preparation time: 10 minutes   Cooking time: 10-15 minutes

**Linguisi,
Chourico or Kielbasa**

Slice sausage into 1/2" rounds. Arrange on a baking sheet and bake at 350° for 10-15 minutes. Serve with Dijon-Horseradish Sauce.

Sauce: Combine equal amounts of Dijon mustard and horseradish. Thin with a small amount of soured cream.

Salmon-Stuffed Cherry Tomatoes

Comments: Attractive and unusual.

Preparation time: 30 minutes

24 cherry tomatoes	1/4 tsp. Worcestershire sauce
3 slices Nova Scotia smoked salmon	1 tsp. chives, finely chopped
3-oz. pkg. cream cheese, softened	parsley for garnish

Core and remove pulp and seeds from tomatoes. Turn upside down on paper towels and drain for several hours in the refrigerator. Mince salmon and stir in cheese. Add Worcestershire sauce and chives. Stuff mixture into tomatoes, and top each with a parsley leaf.

Shrimp Pate

Comments: Subtle, simple and elegant!

Preparation time: 10 minutes

2-oz. flat anchovy fillets	4 drops Tabasco
1 lb. shrimp, cooked	1/2 tbsp. capers
1/4 cup butter, softened	salt and pepper to taste
1/4 cup dry white wine	

Wash and dry anchovies; place in a blender with remaining ingredients. Blend until a smooth paste is formed. Adjust seasonings; chill thoroughly and serve on unsalted crackers.

Shrimp Provencale

Comments: Too simple to be so good!

Preparation time: 20 minutes   Cooking time: 15 minutes

2 lbs. uncooked jumbo shrimp	2-4 cloves garlic, minced
1 tomato, cut in chunks	2 tbsp. parsley, chopped
1/3 cup olive oil	1 tbsp. soy sauce

Clean uncooked shrimp, place in collander and rinse well with cold water. Put shrimp and tomato in heavy skillet. Add olive oil, garlic, parsley and soy sauce. Bake, uncovered at 450° until shrimp turns pink — about 10-15 minutes. Serve immediately after cooking.

Note: May be prepared early in the day and stored, uncooked, in the refrigerator until serving time.

Marinated Shrimp

Comments: Great for a summer picnic!

Preparation time: 10 minutes
(allow for 48 hours' refrigeration)

6 white onions	1-1/2 tsp. salt
4 lbs. shrimp, cooked	4 tsp. celery seed
8 bay leaves	3-oz. capers
2 cups olive oil	2 drops Tabasco
1 cup white vinegar	

Combine all ingredients, adding the shrimp last. Marinate in the refrigerator for 48 hours, stirring occasionally.

Soups

Divine Apple Curry Soup

Comments: A great result from ingredients always in stock.

Preparation time: 5 minutes   Cooking time: 5 minutes

10-3/4-oz. can cream of chicken soup
1 15-oz. jar applesauce
13-3/4-oz. can chicken broth
curry powder to taste

Combine all ingredients in a saucepan and heat through. May be served hot or cold.

Note: May be prepared three or four days in advance and refrigerated.

Curried Apricot Soup

Comments: A successful melange of flavours.

Preparation time: 15 minutes   Cooking time: 20 minutes

1 lb. chicken	1 tbsp. curry powder
or pheasant, cooked, boned	(or to taste)
4-5 whole dried apricots,	2 tbsp. flour
cooked and drained	1 cup heavy cream
2-1/2 cups chicken or	4 tbsp. fresh mint, chopped
pheasant stock	2 tbsp. butter

Puree chicken meat and apricots in blender with 1 cup stock. Melt butter in a saucepan and add curry powder; cook, stirring constantly, for 1 minute. Blend in flour and cook for 1 minute longer. Add remaining chicken stock slowly, stirring constantly. Heat just to boiling, then add the puree. Stir in cream and simmer 15 minutes or until thickened. Add mint and cover; leave on lowest heat possible for 2-3 minutes. Serve immediately.

Note: Soup may be prepared up to the addition of cream and stored or frozen. Add cream when reheating.

Asparagus Soup

Comments: Fine served hot or cold!

Preparation time: 30 minutes   Cooking time: 10 minutes

1-1/2 lbs. fresh asparagus   13-3/4 oz. can of chicken broth
1 heavy tsp. onion, minced   1-1/2 cups of light cream
1 tsp. salt   dash white pepper

Break off asparagus stalks where they snap easily; discard tough ends. Wash stalks well. Cut asparagus crosswise into one inch pieces. Place the asparagus in a medium saucepan with onion, salt, and 3/4 cup of chicken broth; cover and boil gently until the asparagus is tender, about ten minutes. Place in blender and blend until smooth. Stir in remaining broth, cream and pepper. Heat if soup is to be served hot; chill, if to be served cold.

Cream of Broccoli Soup

SERVES 8

Comments: A good French country soup — delicious hot or cold.

Preparation time: 45 minutes   Cooking time: 35-40 minutes

6 cups chicken broth   1 leek, chopped
1-1/2-2 lbs. fresh broccoli   1 bay leaf
1 large potato, peeled   1 whole clove
  and chopped   1/4 cup heavy cream
1 stalk celery, chopped

Combine all ingredients except cream in a large saucepan. Simmer until vegetables are soft, about 35-40 minutes. Remove spices and mash vegetables. Puree the vegetables in a blender, adding more chicken stock if the mixture is too thick. Reheat the puree just before serving and swirl in cream. Do not boil. Season with salt and pepper to taste and serve immediately.

Note: Prepare vegetable base early in the day and let stand for a few hours.

Chicken Lemon Soup

Comments: Sophisticated results with a minimum of effort.

Preparation time: 15 minutes   Cooking time: 20-30 minutes

2 quarts chicken stock   1/2 cup Sauterne
1/2 cup butter   3 egg yolks
2/3 cup uncooked rice   juice of two lemons
1 tsp. powdered chicken stock   parsley, finely chopped
          lemon slices for garnish

Combine the chicken stock and rice, and cook until the rice is tender. Add the butter, powdered chicken stock and wine and simmer gently for 20-30 minutes. In a separate bowl, beat egg yolks and lemon juice until frothy. Just before serving, combine 1 cup of hot soup with the egg lemon mixture and stir briskly with a wire whisk. Add mixture to the rest of the soup. Serve immediately, garnished with thin slices of lemon or chopped parsley.

Clams en Gelee

Comments: A refreshing first course.

Preparation time: 30 minutes

> 2 13-oz. cans red madrilene
> 12-oz. minced clams, drained
> 1 cup celery, finely chopped
> plain yogurt
> parsley, finely chopped

Pour madrilene into a large bowl and refrigerate until nearly set. Fold in clams and chopped celery. Refrigerate until firm. Serve in small bowls or soup cups, topped with plain yogurt and parsley.

Shellfishly Good Clam Chowder

YIELD: 8-10 cups

Comments: A highly-prized recipe! Equally good as a main course or as a prelude to prime ribs.

Preparation time: 20 minutes   Cooking time: 20 minutes

1-2 large onions, chopped
1 bottle clam juice
12-oz. minced clams*
6-oz. whole clams*

reserve liquid

4 large raw potatoes,
 pared and diced
2-3 tbsp. butter
4 cups milk
2 cups medium or heavy cream

Saute onion in butter in a deep kettle until transparent. Add the bottled clam juice plus the liquid from the clams. Add potatoes and cook until the potatoes are just tender. Add remaining ingredients and bring to the boiling point. Refrigerate overnight. Heat before serving.

Hester's Crab Soup

YIELD: 3 QUARTS

Comments: Hats off to Hester!

Preparation time: 15 minutes   Cooking time: 10 minutes

1 lb. lump crabmeat
2 10-3/4 oz. cans cream of celery soup
10-3/4 oz. can cream of tomato soup
10-3/4 can crab soup or shrimp soup

5-1/4 cups milk
3 oz. cream cheese
  with chives
1/2 tsp. Accent
1 cup sherry

Melt the cream cheese in top of double boiler. Add the remaining ingredients and blend until smooth. Heat through, but do not boil. Add sherry just before serving.

Note: Can be prepared without sherry and frozen.

Cream of Cucumber Soup

Comments: Always fresh — cucumbers are available
year-round.

Preparation time: 10 minutes   Cooking time: 30 minutes

1 medium onion, chopped
5 cucumbers, peeled, seeded
   and chopped
1/2 cup butter
1-1/2 quarts hot beef or
   chicken stock

2 cups hot milk
1 cup light cream
chives, chopped
1/2 cup flour
salt and pepper

Saute the onions and cucumber in butter. When soft, add the flour and blend thoroughly to form a roux. Add the hot stock and simmer for 15 minutes. Add the hot milk and simmer for an additional 10 minutes. Remove from heat, place in blender and blend on high speed for 30 seconds (or rub through finest possible sieve). Add cream; season with salt and pepper. Serve immediately or chill and serve cold. Garnish with chopped chives.

Pressed Cucumber Soup

Comments: A standby for the chef who is also a gardener.

Preparation time: 20 minutes

2 large cucumbers, peeled and seeded	3 tbsp. lemon juice
1-1/4 tsp. salt	3/4 tsp. chives, chopped
1/4 tsp. pepper	2 cups soured cream
1 tsp. sugar	1-3/4 cups milk
	cucumber slices for garnish

Shred cucumbers into a large bowl. Add the salt, pepper and sugar and toss gently. Place a smaller bowl on top of the shredded cucumbers to press out the juice but do not drain. Chill at least 2 hours. Stir in lemon juice, chives, soured cream and milk. Garnish with slices of cucumber. Serve ice cold.

Fish Chowder

Comments: A rich, traditional New England chowder.

Preparation time: 30 minutes   Cooking time: 30 minutes

3″ cube salt pork, diced
5 lbs. whole haddock, cut for chowder
2 cups potatoes, cooked and diced
1 lb. onions, chopped

3 cups milk
1 cup light cream
2 cups fish stock

Cover fish with cold water and bring to a boil. Immediately turn off heat and let stand until cool enough to handle. Remove fish from stock; skin and bone, leaving fish in large chunks. Saute salt pork until brown and crisp; remove from pan and saute the onions in the salt pork drippings. Combine the fish, 2 cups of the fish stock, potatoes, onions, milk, cream and salt pork. Add salt and pepper to taste and heat to serving temperature.

Nantucket Fish Chowder

SERVES 12

Comments: As with all chowders, this improves with age. Make it the day before!

Preparation time: 45 minutes   Cooking time: 35-45 minutes

4-5 lbs. whole striped bass or
  other chowder fish
1 pkg. seasoned
  dry stuffing mix
3 large onions, chopped
3 tbsp. butter
1-1/2 quarts milk
1 cup heavy cream

2 cups dry white wine
2 cups water
2 cups light cream
1 bay leaf
salt and pepper to taste
1/2 cup parsley, chopped
3 tbsp. cornstarch

Combine the water, wine, bay leaf, salt and pepper; poach fish in the mixture until it flakes (about 15-20 minutes). Remove fish from stock; remove head, tail, skin and bones carefully, leaving fish in large chunks. Strain stock if necessary, then boil to reduce volume to 2 cups. Prepare stuffing as directed on package. Saute the onion in the butter and add to the stuffing. Combine the cornstarch with approximately 1/4 cup of the fish stock; stir to form a smooth paste, then add the the rest of the fish stock. Add remaining ingredients and reserved fish to the stock, bring to a boil and simmer for 10-15 minutes. Add more milk if desired. Refrigerate overnight. Reheat over low heat. Do not boil.

Portuguese Fish Chowder

Comments: Sausage is a super addition.

Preparation time: 30 minutes   Cooking time: 30 minutes

1 large onion, chopped
2 tbsp. butter
2 cups raw potatoes, diced
1 lb. haddock, skinned
  and boned
1 cup water
2 cups milk

16-oz. can creamed corn
1 tsp. salt
1/2 tsp. pepper
3/4 cup carrots, sliced
1/2 lb. chourico (Portuguese
  sausage), cut in 1/2" slices
13-oz. can evaporated milk

Saute the sausage and onion in butter until sausage is cooked through. Drain and reserve. Combine the potatoes, carrots, fish and water. Cover and simmer for 30 minutes, or until the fish flakes easily and potatoes and carrots are tender. Add remaining ingredients and heat to serving temperature.

Rich Man's Seafood Chowder

Comments: Cognac is the crowning touch!

Preparation time: 30 minutes   Cooking time: 30 minutes

1 cup onion, finely chopped	1 pint clams, shelled
4 tbsp. butter	1 pint scallops
2 cups raw potatoes, diced	1 lb. crabmeat
2-3 cups clam, oyster or fish stock	1 lb. shrimp, cleaned and deveined
6 cups milk	1/2 cup butter
salt and pepper, to taste	1/2 cup cognac
1 tsp. thyme	parsley, chopped
1 pint oysters, shelled	paprika

Saute onion in the butter until softened, but not browned. Add potatoes, cover with stock and simmer until potatoes are tender (add extra water if necessary). Add milk and heat to boiling. Season to taste with salt, pepper, thyme and paprika. Just before serving, add the shellfish and cook for 4 minutes or until fish is tender. Add butter and cognac; place in serving bowls and garnish with parsley and paprika. Serve immediately.

Note: A pint of heavy cream will add richness.

Cold Curry Soup

Comments: A tangy twist for an old stand-by.

Preparation time: 15 minutes

1/4 tsp. sugar	5 tbsp. mayonnaise
1 small onion, quartered	1 tsp. parsley, minced
1-1/2 tsp. salt	1 tsp. curry powder
1/4 tsp. pepper	7 large tomatoes

Peel tomatoes and puree in blender with onion, salt, pepper, and sugar. Chill in refrigerator for several hours. Just before serving, blend in the mayonnaise, parsley and curry powder. Serve well chilled.

Jeweled Madrilene

SERVES 4

Comments: Caviar adds a touch of luxury.

Preparation time: 10 minutes

2 13-oz. cans madrilene	1/2 cup soured cream
4 oz. black caviar (lumpfish)	lemon wedges
1 tbsp. onion, grated	

Spoon caviar into bowls or soup cups. Cover with chilled madrilene and refrigerate. Combine the soured cream and onion. Just before serving, put a dollop of the soured cream mixture on the top of each serving, and garnish with a lemon wedge.

View of the Boston Lighthouse
by William Burgis, 1729
Courtesy of the Mariners Museum, Newport News, Virginia

Black Mushroom Soup

Comments: An easy-to-prepare broth that tastes as if it
took hours.

Preparation time: 10 minutes   Cooking time: 1 hour

1/2 lb. fresh mushrooms, thinly sliced	**1 soup can cold water**
2 10-3/4 oz. cans beef consomme	**salt and pepper to taste**

Combine mushrooms, consomme and water; bring to a boil and simmer uncovered for 1 hour. Season to taste with salt and pepper. Strain to remove mushrooms before serving, saving some for garnish.

Variation: Just before serving, add diced cooked pork, a few sliced scallions and a few shredded spinach leaves.

Cream of Onion Soup

Comments: A delicate flavour.

Preparation time: 30 minutes   Cooking time: 30 minutes

1 lb. onions, thinly sliced	salt and pepper to taste
1/4 cup butter	2 egg yolks
5 cups chicken broth	2 tbsp. Parmesan cheese, grated
1/4 tsp. mace	1 cup heavy cream
1/2 tsp. nutmeg	fresh parsley, chopped

Melt butter and cook onions until tender, not brown. Add the chicken broth and simmer gently for 30 minutes (covered). Puree the onion mixture in a blender; return to heat and season with mace, nutmeg, salt and pepper. In a separate bowl, blend the egg yolks, parmesan cheese and cream. Add a little of the hot mixture to the egg mixture and blend until smooth; combine with the rest of the hot soup. Heat slowly to serving temperature. Do not boil. Garnish with fresh chopped parsley.

Polish Cabbage Soup

SERVES 4-6

Comments: Delicious for a supper on a cold winter evening!

Preparation time: 5 minutes   Cooking time: 50 minutes

> 1 Kielbasa sausage (average size)
> 1 small head cabbage, shredded coarsely
> 16-oz. can red kidney beans
> 2-3 medium potatoes, diced

Slice sausage in 1/2-3/4″ slices. Simmer the sausage for 20-30 minutes in just enough water to cover. Add cabbage, potatoes and undrained beans and cook for an additional 20 minutes or until all ingredients are tender. The amounts of cabbage and potatoes may be adjusted to individual tastes.

Note: Keeps well in the refrigerator for a few days.

Cream of Pumpkin Soup

Comments: Very French! The tomato adds a special touch.

Preparation time: 30 minutes   Cooking time: 15 minutes

1/2 cup scallions, sliced
3 tbsp. butter
2 cups cooked pumpkin
   mashed and strained (or one
   16-oz. can)
13-3/4 oz. chicken broth

1 small ripe tomato,
   peeled and chopped
1/2 tsp. salt
freshly ground pepper
1 cup light cream

Saute scallions in butter until transparent. Stir in pumpkin, 1 cup of the chicken broth, tomato, salt and pepper. Bring to a boil and simmer for 15 minutes. Place pumpkin mixture in blender and puree. Return to saucepan and add cream and remaining chicken broth. Heat to serving temperature. Do not boil.

Note: Equally delicious served cold.

Sausage and Bean Soup

SERVES 4

Comments: Served with black bread and German wine this is ideal for a "tailgate party" or a winter supper.

Preparation time: 20 minutes   Cooking time: 1 hour

10-3/4 oz. can black bean soup
10-3/4 oz. can bacon and bean soup
2 soup cans water
1 lb. "hot" flavour
   sausage meat*
1 medium onion, chopped

Worcestershire sauce to taste
Tabasco to taste
1-2 cloves garlic, mashed
salt and pepper to taste
1 medium green pepper, chopped
1 stalk celery, chopped

or hot Italian sausage, removed from casing.

Break up sausage meat in a large skillet and cook until browned and crumbly. Drain and set aside. Brown the onions, peppers and celery in the sausage drippings. Set aside. Pour the soup and water into a large saucepan and heat. Add remaining ingredients and season to taste. Cook over medium heat, stirring occasionally, for 30 minutes.

Scallop and Artichoke Soup

SERVES 4-6

Comments: Very subtle—from Lacy's in London.

Preparation time: 15-20 minutes   Cooking time: 15-20 minutes

1 pkg. frozen artichoke hearts,   1/2 lb. fresh scallops, chopped
   defrosted   salt to taste
4 tbsp. butter   1/8 tsp. lemon juice
2 tbsp. flour   1 cup heavy cream
2 cups chicken broth

Saute artichokes in butter for a few minutes; add flour and blend well. Add chicken stock and simmer until artichokes are tender. Puree mixture in blender. Return to low heat and add the chopped scallops. Heat until scallops are no longer opaque. Add cream and lemon juice. Heat to serving temperature. Do not boil.

Seviche Soup

Comments: Our version of a Spanish specialty.

Preparation time: 30 minutes

1/2 lb. scallops
1/2 cup lime juice
1/3 cup onion, chopped
1 tsp. salt
1-1/2 cups tomato juice

1 can chicken broth
1 tsp. fresh coriander, minced
  or parsley
2 tbsp. chili peppers, minced
  (seeds removed)

Coarsely chop the scallops; mix with the lime juice, chopped onion and salt. Cover and chill overnight. Combine scallop mixture with remaining ingredients, adding peppers to taste. Serve chilled. Garnish with coriander or parsley.

Both Ways Farm Sorrel Soup

Comments: A delectable use for a little-known green.

Preparation time: 30 minutes   Cooking time: 20 minutes

1/2 cup onions, minced	1/2 tsp. salt
5 tbsp. butter	3 tbsp. flour
3-1/2 cups packed fresh sorrel	5-1/2 cups boiling chicken stock
(washed and dried)*	2 egg yolks
	1/2 cup whipping cream

Spinach or watercress may be substituted.

Saute the onions in 3 tbsp. of the butter until transparent. Stir in the sorrel and salt; cook over low heat until leaves are tender and wilted. Sprinkle in flour and stir for 5 more minutes. Remove from heat and beat in the boiling stock; return to heat and simmer for an additional 5 minutes. Puree the soup in a blender, then return to heat. Combine the egg yolks and cream with 1 cup of the soup; blend thoroughly then add to the rest of the soup. Stir soup over moderate heat for one or two minutes. Do not boil. Swirl the remaining butter on the top of the soup just before serving.

Tangerine Tomato Bouillon

SERVES 6-8

Comments: Good for tailgate picnics or a morning meeting.

Preparation time: 10 minutes   Cooking time: 5 minutes

1 quart tomato juice
2 10-3/4 oz. cans beef bouillon, undiluted
1-2 tsp. "Jane's Krazy Mixed-Up Salt"

8-oz. can frozen tangerine
  juice, undiluted*
1/2 cup sherry, optional
orange juice may be substituted

Heat the tomato juice, bouillon and salt. Simmer 10 minutes. Add the tangerine juice and sherry if desired just before serving. Heat but do not boil.

General Howe Evacuating Boston
by M. A. Wagman and J. Godfrey, 1861
Courtesy of the Bostonian Society, Old State House, Boston, Massachusetts

Soups

Cream of Tomato Soup

Comments: Home-made tomato soup — an American classic.

Preparation time: 1 hour   Cooking time: 45-50 minutes

12 tbsp. butter	3 tbsp. tomato paste
2 tbsp. olive oil	1/4 cup flour
2 cups onion, thinly sliced	3-3/4 cups chicken broth
2 sprigs fresh thyme	1 tsp. sugar
(or 1/2 tsp. dry)	1 cup heavy cream
4 basil leaves, chopped	croutons for garnish
(or 1/2 tsp. dry)	salt and pepper to taste
2-1/2 lbs. fresh ripe tomatoes,	
cored	

Combine the olive oil with 8 tbsp. of the butter in a large pot. Add onion, thyme, basil, salt and pepper. Cook over low heat until the onion is transparent. Add the tomatoes and tomato paste; blend well and simmer for 10 minutes. Combine the flour and 1/4 cup of the chicken broth; blend until smooth. Stir the flour mixture into the soup, then add the remaining chicken broth and simmer for 30 minutes, stirring frequently. Strain stock through sieve, discarding tomato peels. Return mixture to the stove and stir in the sugar and cream. Warm to serving temperature. Do not boil. Add remaining butter to soup just before serving. Garnish with croutons.

Tomato Onion Soup

Comments: An old Vermont recipe dating back to the days when "butter the size of an egg" was a common measure and "top milk" was on every quart.

Preparation time: 15 minutes   Cooking time: 2 hours

2-1/2 lbs. fresh tomatoes or
1 large can tomatoes (1 lb. 12 oz.)
3 onions, sliced
3 tbsp. uncooked rice
2 quarts warm water

butter the size of an egg (3 tbsp.)
1 cup top milk
  (use light cream)
salt to taste

Combine all ingredients except cream; bring to a boil and simmer for 2 hours. Add cream gradually and salt to taste. Better the second day.

Vichysquash

Comments: A variation of a traditional favorite.

Preparation time: 15 minutes   Cooking time: 30 minutes

1 lb. butternut squash, peeled and seeded	2 tbsp. brown sugar
	salt and pepper to taste
4 cups chicken stock	light cream
1 medium onion, chopped	soured cream and seasonal herbs for garnish

Cook squash with the onion in the chicken stock until tender. Add brown sugar, salt and pepper. Puree in blender. Before serving, thin with light cream. Place a dollop of soured cream on top of soup and garnish with herbs.

Zucchini Soup

Comments: A smooth and creamy summer specialty.

Preparation time: 10-15 minutes   Cooking time: 15-20 minutes

1 small onion, quartered
1-1/2 cups chicken broth
1/2 cup potatoes,
   cooked and diced
1 cup zucchini, cooked

1/4 cup fresh chopped parsley
1/2 tsp. celery salt
1 cup light cream
1/2 cup soured cream (optional)

Puree the onion and potatoes with 1/2 cup of the broth in a blender. Add the remaining broth, cooked zucchini, parsley, celery salt, cream and soured cream (if desired). Chill well before serving.

Luncheon Dishes

Mock Quiche Canadienne

SERVES 4-6

Comments: Though it is similar to a quiche, it puffs a little like a souffle.

Preparation time: 15 minutes   Cooking time: 45-50 minutes

6 slices Canadian bacon	1/3 tsp. salt
1/2 lb. Swiss cheese, grated	1/4 tsp. ground nutmeg
3 eggs, beaten	1/2 cup Parmesan cheese, grated
2 cups light cream	parsley sprigs for garnish

Arrange slices of bacon in a shallow 1-1/2 quart baking dish. Combine all remaining ingredients except parsley and pour over the bacon. Set the baking dish in a roasting pan filled with 1″ hot water. Bake at 350° for 45-50 minutes, or until a knife inserted in center comes out clean. Garnish with parsley and serve immediately. May also be reheated.

Note: Sliced ham may be substituted for the bacon.

Cheese and Wine Casserole

SERVES 6

Comments: Serve with salad for a delightful luncheon or Sunday night supper.

Preparation time: 15 minutes   Cooking time: 30 minutes

1/2 lb. Gruyere cheese, grated	6 eggs
1-1/2 cups dry white wine	1/2 cup heavy cream
6 slices bread, trimmed	1/2 cup chicken bouillon
6 tbsp. butter	1/4 tsp. dry mustard
1 garlic clove, crushed	1 tsp. paprika

Cream butter and garlic together and spread on bread. Arrange bread buttered side down in a single layer in a shallow baking dish. Beat eggs until frothy; beat in cream and add remaining ingredients. Pour over bread. Bake in a 350° oven for 30 minutes or until puffed and brown.

Crepes Benedict

Comments: An elegant version of Eggs Benedict.

Preparation time: 20 minutes crepes
                           20 minutes eggs
                           10 minutes sauce

15 eggs	vegetable oil
1 cup flour	2 egg yolks
1-1/2 cups milk	2 tbsp. lemon juice
salt	1/2 cup butter, melted
1 tbsp. parsley, finely chopped	dash cayenne

Poach 12 eggs, leaving them slightly undercooked, and drop immediately into a bowl of ice water after cooking. Refrigerate. For the crepes: combine the flour, 3 eggs, milk, salt and parsley and mix until the batter is smooth and the consistency of heavy cream. Do not beat. Refrigerate the batter for one hour, if possible. Place 1 tbsp. oil in a skillet. Be sure the pan is hot and well-oiled before making each additional crepe. When the skillet is hot, pour in 2 tbsp. of batter and tilt the pan quickly so that the batter covers the entire pan. Cook for one minute on the first side; turn with spatula and cook about 30 seconds on the second side. The crepes can be refrigerated or frozen, but they must be warmed before filling. Just before serving, prepare a hollandaise sauce by placing the egg yolks and lemon juice in a blender. Both should be at room temperature. Blend at high speed until thick; add the melted butter very slowly. Blend until all the butter is absorbed. Add salt and cayenne to taste. If the eggs have been poached ahead of time, reheat by submerging in boiling water for 30 seconds. Place a slice of ham and poached egg on each crepe; fold crepe and place in a buttered shallow baking dish. When all of the crepes are assembled, top with hollandaise and broil as far away from the heat source as possible until the hollandaise is bubbly. Serve immediately.

The Bloody Massacre Perpetrated in King Street
by Paul Revere II, 1770
Courtesy of the Museum of Fine Arts, Boston, Massachusetts

Luncheon Dishes

Stuffed Eggplant

SERVES 4-6

Comments: A mid-Eastern favorite, perfect with a salad and Syrian bread.

Preparation time: 45 minutes   Cooking time: 1 hour

3 eggplants	1 clove garlic, minced
1 to 1-1/2 lbs. lean ground beef	1 onion, diced
2 tbsp. olive oil	6 tomatoes, chopped
1/2 tsp. rosemary	1/4 cup fresh parsley
1/2 tsp. salt	3/4 cup bread crumbs
1/2 tsp. freshly ground pepper	1/2 cup Parmesan cheese, grated

Halve eggplants lengthwise and bake in a greased pan for 30 minutes at 350°. While the eggplant is baking, saute the onion and garlic in 1 tbsp. oil; cook until onion is transparent. Add the beef and continue cooking until it loses its redness. Do not overcook. Set aside. Combine the bread crumbs, grated cheese and parsley; set aside. After baking, scoop out the seeds of the eggplant and discard; remove all but 1/2 inch of pulp from each eggplant; coarsely chop the scooped out pulp and combine with the tomatoes, salt, pepper and rosemary. Toss lightly to mix. Fill the eggplant shells in layers, beginning with a layer of beef mixture, followed by the tomato mixture and topped with the bread crumb mixture. Sprinkle 1/2 tsp. of oil over the top of each shell and bake for 30 minutes at 350°.

Melanzana a la Parmigiana

Comments: Good for a hearty luncheon or supper.

Preparation time: 30 minutes   Cooking time: 20 minutes

1 large eggplant
2 cups bread crumbs
1 tsp. parsley, chopped
2 cloves garlic, minced
2 tbsp. tomato paste

1/2 cup olive oil
1/2 lb. Mozarella cheese, sliced
1 #2 can tomatoes (1 lb. 4 oz.)
1/2 cup Parmesan cheese, grated
dash basil and oregano

Blend tomatoes, tomato paste, 2 tbsp. olive oil and a pinch of salt in a saucepan, and simmer 20 minutes. Wash and dry eggplant; slice 1/2" thick. Cover eggplant with hot water and let stand for 5 minutes. Drain and dry. Fry eggplant slices in the remaining oil for 3 minutes, until soft and light brown, adding extra olive oil if needed. Drain and set aside. Combine bread crumbs, Parmesan cheese, parsley, garlic, basil and oregano. Arrange ingredients in layers in a flat baking dish: first a layer of eggplant, followed by bread crumb mixture, tomatoes and slices of mozzarella. Bake at 350° for 20 minutes or until cheese melts.

Roquefort Mousse Extraordinaire

Comments: For Roquefort addicts! Lovely filled with lobster or any seafood salad.

Preparation time: 30 minutes

1 envelope unflavoured gelatin	2 tbsp. pimento, minced
1/4 cup lemon juice	1 tbsp. capers, minced
1 cup boiling water	1 tsp. onion, minced
1/4 lb. Roquefort cheese	salt and freshly ground pepper
1 cup cucumber, grated	1 cup heavy cream, whipped
4 tbsp. parsley, minced	

Soften the gelatin in the lemon juice; dissolve in boiling water. Thoroughly mash the cheese and combine with the cucumbers, parsley, pimento, capers and onion. Add salt and pepper to taste. Stir in the dissolved gelatin. Chill until the mixture begins to set; fold in the whipped cream. Spread the mousse into a lightly oiled 6-cup ring mold and chill for four hours or until completely firm. Unmold onto a chilled serving platter and fill with seafood salad.

Luncheon Dishes

Tomatoes à la Shrimp

Comments: Perfect for land-locked seafood lovers.

Preparation time: 15 minutes

1 large firm tomato per person	tarragon
canned tiny shrimp	freshly ground pepper
mayonnaise	fresh parsley
light cream	lemon juice

Remove tops from tomatoes and scoop out the seeds. Invert shells on paper towels and let drain for 15-20 minutes. Thin the mayonnaise with a little cream. Add the shrimp and season to taste. Fill the tomato shells and chill. Serve on lettuce.

Cold Stuffed Zucchini

Comments: Crisp and cool with a European flavour.

Preparation time: 30 minutes   Cooking time: 5-8 minutes

3 medium zucchini
lemon juice
olive oil
4 tbsp. tuna fish
    (packed in oil)
1/2 cup black olives,
    finely sliced
1-1/2 cups mayonnaise

1 tbsp. capers, drained
1 clove garlic, mashed
2 tsp. anchovy paste
salt and freshly ground pepper
thinly sliced onion
fresh parsley, chopped

Poach the zucchini in boiling water for 5-8 minutes, or until firm but tender. Split in half lengthwise. Remove the seeds, leaving the shell intact; sprinkle each half with a little lemon juice and olive oil. Combine the tuna, olives and 1 tbsp. mayonnaise in a small bowl. Add a dash of lemon and blend well. Fill the zucchini shells with the tuna mixture. Combine the remaining mayonnaise, capers, garlic, and anchovy paste; season with salt and pepper. Pour the mayonnaise mixture over each of the zucchini shells and refrigerate until serving time. Garnish with slices of onion and parsley.

Fish and Shellfish

Baked Stuffed Bluefish

Comments: Simply superb! Serve with Tarragon Tomatoes.

Preparation time: 20 minutes   Cooking time: 40-50 minutes

1 whole bluefish (4-5 lbs.),
  boned and cleaned
  with head and tail intact
6 medium mushrooms, sliced
2 or 3 fresh tomatoes,
  quartered
parsley, chopped

2 green peppers, seeded and
  sliced
3 tbsp. butter, softened
additional butter and olive oil
1 lemon
1 cup dry white wine or
  vermouth

Butter the cavity of the fish with some of the softened butter. Saute the mushrooms, tomatoes and green peppers in a combination of olive oil and butter. Combine the three and add the parsley. Stuff the fish with the mixture and sprinkle with bread crumbs. Sew the open edge of the cavity and place the fish in a buttered baking dish. Make six diagonal slits in the top of the fish; butter the outside of the fish and place six slices of lemon (1/8" thick) partially under the skin in the slits. Bake at 350° for 40-50 minutes, or until the fish flakes readily. Baste frequently during baking with 1 cup of white wine or dry vermouth.

Note: The fish may also be cooked on a charcoal grill. Wrap the fish with foil and pour the wine over the fish before sealing. The coals should be hot. Turn the fish frequently, cooking for about 40 minutes.

Fish and Shellfish

Clambake

Comments: The greatest cookout of them all!

Preparation time: 2 and a half hours   Cooking time: 1 hour

Dig a shallow circular pit in the sand well above the high tide mark. The pit should be 10″ deep and 3 feet across. Line with large smooth rocks. Build a fire of dry hardwood to cover the entire bottom and keep it blazing for at least 2 hours to thoroughly heat the rocks. To test the rocks, drip a little water on them. If they sizzle and steam, they are ready. Rake out the fire and put a 6″ layer of wet seaweed directly on the red hot rocks. Place in layers on top of the seaweed any or all of the following:

> clams* (10-12 washed and unopened per person) place in
>   a potato sack or pillow case
> lobsters* (1 per person)
> corn in the husk (soaked in salt water for an hour)
> potatoes (washed and unpeeled)
> split chicken (1/2 per person) wrapped in cheese cloth
> frankfurters or sausages (2 per person)

Cover all with a heavy canvas anchored with rocks. Allow to steam for an hour. Serve with melted butter, a keg of beer and watermelon.

*For those unable to get fresh lobsters and clams locally, several companies in Maine will ship all the necessary supplies, even the seaweed, to any part of the country.

Fish and Shellfish   75

Clam Fritters

Comments: Light, tasty morsels.

Preparation time: 5-10 minutes   Cooking time: 5 minutes

1 cup flour
1 tsp. baking powder
1/2 tsp. salt
2 (7 oz.) cans minced clams

1 egg
1 tbsp. vegetable oil
dash lemon juice
oil for cooking
bacon fat (optional)

Drain clams, reserving 1/2 cup of the liquid. Mix clam liquid with egg and beat. Stir in flour and baking powder, then add the clams, oil, salt and lemon juice. Drop by the spoonful into deep fat (half oil, half bacon fat if desired), and cook until browned. Drain and salt lightly. Serve immediately.

Cold Curried Clams Cohasset

SERVES 8

Comments: Marvelous for a summer luncheon or an elegant picnic.

Preparation time: 10 minutes

> 2 quarts steamer clams, cooked   2 tbsp. Dijon mustard
> 1/2 - 3/4 cup curried mayonnaise

Follow the directions for steaming clams under Clams Linguine (page 78), removing their shells and neck sheathings. Chill the clams in a bowl filled with broth from the steaming procedure, using enough to cover the clams. Drain the clams when chilled (after 3 or 4 hours). Blend the mayonnaise and mustard in a separate bowl. Add that mixture to the clams and stir to blend. Serve on lettuce.

Curried Mayonnaise

YIELD: 1 CUP

Preparation time: 10 minutes

> 1 egg yolk   3/4 cup olive oil
> salt and ground pepper to taste   1/2-1 tsp. cayenne
> 1 tsp. Dijon mustard   1/2-1 tsp. curry powder
> 1 tsp. lemon juice

Place the egg yolk in a mixing bowl and add salt and pepper, mustard and lemon juice. Gradually add the oil while beating vigorously with a wire whisk. When half of the oil has been added, the remaining oil can be added more rapidly. Add more salt to taste and the curry powder and cayenne. Chill.

Clams Linguine

Comments: Best we've had since dinner at El Pescatore, Roma!

1-2 quarts steamer clams	1/2 lb. linguine
1/2 cup olive oil	1 bottle beer
6 tbsp. butter	4 tbsp. parsley, finely chopped
6 large cloves garlic, chopped	1/3 hot pepper, chopped
3 tsp. salt	freshly ground pepper

Steam thoroughly cleaned clams in a kettle containing 1/2 inch water and the bottle of beer until shells open. Reserve broth. Remove clams from their shells, discarding necks' sheathing. Slowly heat olive oil and butter in a skillet. Add garlic and saute for 5 minutes, or until golden brown. Remove immediately from heat. Add 1-1/2 cups of the reserved clam broth, salt, pepper, chopped parsley, and hot peppers. Bring to a boil slowly and simmer, uncovered, for 10 minutes. Meanwhile, boil linguine "al dente." Add clams to the sauce 3 minutes before the linguine is ready. Pour over linguine and serve immediately in soup bowls.

Note: it is important that the clams be simmered only 3 minutes. If cooked longer, they will become tough and rubbery.

Herring Salad

Comments: A traditional Scandinavian favorite.

Preparation time: 30 minutes

2 jars Vita marinated herring, chopped
1-1/2 cups boiled potatoes, diced
1-1/2 cups pickled beets, diced
1/2 cup apples, diced

1/4 cup onions, chopped
soured cream or yogurt
salt and pepper to taste
hard boiled eggs
parsley

Mix all ingredients together, adding enough soured cream to form thick consistency. Garnish with sliced hard-boiled eggs and parsley. Serve chilled.

Note: May be served as a salad or light luncheon dish. Equally good on crackers.

Scandinavian Fish Bake

Comments: This Swedish recipe can be altered by stuffing the fillets with shrimp or crab.

Preparation time: 30 minutes   Cooking time: 30 minutes

8-10 small yellow onions	1 chicken bouillon cube
1 lb. cod fillets	salt
salt	white pepper
4 tbsp. butter	1/2 cup light cream
2-1/2 tbsp. flour	1/4 cup Parmesan cheese,
3/4 cup milk	grated
1/2 cup water	dill for garnish

Peel and slice onions. Place in small skillet. Add 2 tbsp. water and simmer, covered, until onions are soft and transparent. Remove cover and add 2 tbsp. of the butter. Cook until the water evaporates. Line a shallow baking dish with onions and cover with the cod fillets. Salt lightly. Set aside. Melt remaining 2 tbsp. of butter, add flour and stir until smooth. Add remaining ingredients (except parmesan), including bouillon cube dissolved in remaining water, and stir constantly until thickened. Pour sauce over fish. Sprinkle the top with parmesan and bake at 350° for 25-30 minutes. Garnish with chopped dill and serve with boiled potatoes.

Note: Frozen cod or other white fish may be substituted.

Haddock Stuffed with Oysters

Comments: A sublime and beautiful presentation.

Preparation time: 15 minutes   Cooking time: 50 minutes

4 lbs. haddock fillets	1 egg, slightly beaten
salt	1 cup buttered crumbs
1 pint oysters	hollandaise sauce
lemon juice	lemon wedges
	fresh parsley

Sprinkle fillets with salt and brush with lemon juice. Dip oysters in buttered crumbs, seasoned with salt and pepper. Place one fillet in the bottom of a greased baking pan. Cover the fillet with a layer of oysters. Top with the other fillet. Brush with egg and cover with bread crumbs. Bake for 40 to 50 minutes in a 350° oven. Remove to a heated platter. Cover with 2-3 cups of hollandaise. Garnish with fresh lemon wedges rolled in fresh parsley flakes.

Note. For appearance, two long fillets are preferable to smaller pieces.

Lobster Shelbourne

SERVES 2-3

Comments: This simple but delicious treat originated with the maitre d'hotel of one of the finest hotels in old-time Atlantic City.

Preparation time: 20 minutes   Cooking time: 20-25 minutes

1 lb. cooked lobster meat
1/4 lb. butter
4 oz. chili sauce

dash Worcestershire sauce
dash or more dry sherry

Melt butter in a saucepan and add all ingredients but lobster. Cook, stirring, until sauce simmers. Add lobster and heat to serving temperature. Do not boil. Serve over rice or toast points.

Mussels Duxbury

Comments: It's great fun to take a pail to a spot where the water runs swiftly and pick your own bucketful.

Preparation time: 30 minutes   Cooking time: 12 minutes

4 dozen mussels
9 tbsp. butter
3 garlic cloves, chopped
1 tbsp. shallots, chopped
   (or 1 small onion, chopped)
1 tbsp. parsley, chopped

1 cup dry white wine
few drops lemon juice
salt and freshly ground pepper
chives or parsley for garnish

Clean mussels by scrubbing thoroughly in a generous amount of water, changing water several times. Combine 2 tbs. butter, shallots, garlic, parsley and wine in a kettle. Add mussels and cook, covered, over high heat for 10 minutes or until the shells are opened wide. Remove mussels from pan, reserving liquid. Arrange the mussels on half-shell in serving dishes. Reduce liquid in pan over high heat to 1/3 its original quantity. Add remaining butter, a few drops of lemon juice, salt and freshly-ground pepper. When butter is melted, pour sauce over mussels. Garnish with chives or parsley.

Note: If a thicker sauce is desired, melt butter and blend in 1/2 tsp. flour before adding it to the mussel liquid.

Oysters à la D'uxelles

Comments: Rich — a must even for those who think they don't like oysters.

Preparation time: 30 minutes   Cooking time: 5 minutes

1 pint oysters	1/2 tsp. salt
2 tbsp. butter	1/2 tsp. lemon juice
2 tbsp. mushrooms, chopped	dash cayenne
2 tbsp. flour	1 egg yolk

Parboil oysters in their own juice and a little extra water until the oysters are plump and the edges begin to curl. Strain, reserving liquid. Add water to make 3/4 cup liquid. Saute mushrooms in butter for 5 minutes. Add flour and then gradually add oyster liquid. Cook for 3 minutes. Add seasonings and oysters. Stir in egg yolk. Stir and cook over medium heat until heated through and slightly thickened. Do not boil. Serve on toast points.

Oysters St. Jacques

SERVES 6

Comments: A traditional first course with an Oriental touch!

Preparation time: 30 minutes   Cooking time: 5 minutes

24 oysters
24 cooked shrimp,
   peeled and deveined
1 5-oz. can water chestnuts,
   sliced
1 4-oz. can mushrooms,
   sliced

3 tbsp. butter
1/3 cup flour
1 cup milk
1 tbsp. sherry
salt and pepper
grated Swiss cheese

Into each of six scallop baking shells, place 4 shrimp, 4 oysters, sliced water chestnuts and sliced mushrooms. Melt butter, and add flour. Stir until smooth, then add milk slowly, stirring constantly. When the sauce is smooth, add sherry and season to taste with salt and pepper. Pour equal amounts of the sauce into each of the shells. Sprinkle with grated cheese and broil until bubbly. Garnish with paprika.

Cape Cod Oyster Dressing

Comments: A traditional New England favorite.

Preparation time: 30 minutes

1 pint oysters, drained and chopped	1/2 cup onion, chopped
3/4 cup celery, diced	1/2 lb. butter
	1 lg. pkg. dry prepared stuffing

Melt butter in a small saucepan. Add celery and onion and simmer until the onion is transparent. Remove from heat. Combine the celery, onion, oysters and 2 cups of hot water with the dry stuffing, and toss gently.

Note: The liquid from the oysters may be substituted for some of the water if a stronger oyster flavour is desired.

Tidewater Scallop

Comments: Reminiscent of Colonial times.

Preparation time: 20 minutes   Cooking time: 30 minutes

6 oz. green noodles cooked al dente	1/2-1 cup onion, chopped dash Tabasco
2 10 oz. cans oyster stew, frozen	1 cup milk 1/4 cup flour
1/2 cup butter	1/4 cup Parmesan cheese, grated
1-2 cup cooked ham, chopped	1/2 pint fresh oysters

Melt 1/4 cup of the butter; add ham and brown, then add onions
and cook until tender. Add stew and Tabasco to the ham and
onion mixture and heat until stew is fully thawed. Melt the remaining butter; stir in flour to form roux. Add milk to the roux
slowly and stir until smooth; combine with the stew. Stir in
oysters and noodles and place the stew in a casserole. Sprinkle
with the Parmesan cheese and bake at 350° for 30 minutes.

Paella

Comments: Delicious concoction — beautiful to behold!

Preparation time: 2 hours   Cooking time: 45 minutes

1/4 lb. lean bacon, diced	1 bay leaf
1 lb. Italian hot sausages	1/2 tsp. thyme
4 tbsp. olive oil	3/4 tsp. oregano
1 cup onions, sliced	salt and pepper
1 cup green peppers, sliced	1 lb. shrimp, peeled and deveined
4 cloves garlic, minced	2 tbsp. lemon juice
6 whole chicken breasts, boned and split	4 quarts boiling salted water
2 cups uncooked rice	4 tomatoes
1/2 cup dry white wine	2 cups green peas, raw
1-1/2 cups beef broth	2 cups garbanzos (chick peas)
1-1/2 cups chicken broth	12 artichoke hearts
1 tsp. saffron	24 mussels, unshucked
1 tbsp. paprika	24 clams, unshucked
1/4 tsp. coriander	1 pimento, diced
	2 oz. pimiento, diced

Simmer Italian sausage in water for 10 minutes. Drain and dice sausage; place sausage and bacon in a skillet with 2 tbsp. olive oil and saute until brown. Add the onions and green peppers and cook slowly for 10 minutes. Remove vegetables and meat from the pan. Brown chicken and garlic in remaining drippings. Remove from the pan. Add the rice to the pan and saute until golden. Add saffron, wine, broth and other seasonings. Bring to a boil, then remove from heat. Place the shrimp in a bowl and toss with the lemon juice, oregano, 2 tbsp. olive oil, salt and pepper. Drop tomatoes into boiling water for 10 seconds; remove, peel, halve, squeeze out juice and seeds and set pulp aside. Butter the bottom and sides of a deep casserole or paella dish. Quarter the chicken breasts and place in the bottom of the casserole. Cover with the bacon, sausages, onions and green peppers. Add half of the rice. Then add the peas, garbanzos, artichoke hearts, tomato pulp, pimiento and the rest of the rice. The casserole may be refrigerated at this point and stored for up to 24 hours. Bake uncovered at 350° for 30 minutes, adding chicken stock as needed. Add the shrimp, mussels and clams in their shells. Steam for 15-30 minutes, until the shells open. Serve at once.

Note: Before starting preparation, scrub shellfish and let stand in several changes of water for an hour or until the sand is out.

The Liberty Tree, 1774, Corner of Essex and Washington Streets
by A. Bowen, 1824
Courtesy of the Bostonian Society, Old State House, Boston, Massachusetts

Fish and Shellfish

Salmon with Cucumber Sauce

Comments: A tradition in New England on the 4th of July.

Preparation time: 25 minutes   Cooking time: 20 minutes

6 salmon steaks	1 tbsp. parsley, minced
2 tbsp. lemon juice	1 tbsp. onion, grated
1 cucumber, unpared	2 tsp. vinegar
1/2 cup soured cream	salt and pepper to taste
1/4 cup mayonnaise	lemon wedges
	lettuce leaves

Boil 1 quart of water with 1-1/2 tsp. salt and 2 tbsp. lemon juice in a large skillet. Add 3 salmon steaks and simmer 10 minutes or until fish is cooked. Repeat with the remaining steaks. Chill. To make sauce: shred enough cucumber to make 1 cup (do not drain); add remaining ingredients and blend well. Chill. Arrange salmon on bed of lettuce just before serving. Serve with cucumber sauce and lemon wedges.

Scallops Chappaquiddick

Comments: "Chappy" is one of New England's best scalloping areas.

Preparation time: 10 minutes   Cooking time: 25 minutes

1 lb. scallops	3 slices of white bread
1/2 cup butter	1 cup light cream
1 cup cracker crumbs	salt and pepper

Wash scallops carefully to remove all sand. Crumb bread in blender. Melt butter and add cracker and bread crumbs. Put a layer of crumbs in a small casserole dish; cover with scallops. Add half the cream and salt and pepper. Repeat layers. Bake at 350° about 25 minutes or until scallops are firm but tender. Serve immediately.

Schrod Anthony

Comments: The perfect treatment for baby cod fish.

Preparation time: 5 minutes   Cooking time: 9-10 minutes

2 lbs. schrod (1/2 lb. per person)   **bread crumbs**
1/2 cup melted butter   **fresh lemon**

Dip schrod in melted butter and bread crumbs. Broil until
cooked through (9-10 minutes). Reserve a little of the melted
butter, add lemon juice to taste and pour over the fish after
cooking. If the fish is thick, it can be placed in a 350° oven and
baked for 5-10 minutes more or until fish is cooked through. Fish
is done when the flesh is no longer transparent, flakes readily,
and is firm to the touch. Garnish with lemon wedges and parsley.

Shrimp and Artichoke Casserole

Comments: Reputedly Adlai Stevenson's favorite.

Preparation time: 20 minutes   Cooking time: 20-30 minutes

6-1/2 tbsp. butter
4-1/2 tbsp. flour
3/4 cup milk
3/4 cup heavy cream
salt and pepper to taste
15 oz. can artichoke hearts,
   drained and halved, or
   1 package frozen (thawed)

1 lb. cooked shrimp,
   peeled and deveined
1/2 lb. fresh mushrooms, sliced
1/4 cup sherry
1 tbsp. Worcestershire sauce
1/4 cup Parmesan cheese, grated
paprika

Preheat oven to 375°. Melt butter and saute mushrooms for 2 minutes. Stir in flour and blend with a whisk. Gradually add cream and milk, stirring constantly. When thickened, add salt and pepper to taste. Arrange artichoke hearts and shrimp in the bottom of a casserole. Add sherry and Worcestershire sauce to the mushroom mixture, then pour sauce over the shrimp and artichokes. Sprinkle with cheese and paprika. Bake uncovered for 20-30 minutes. Serve over rice.

Shrimp India

Comments: The curry seasoning is subtle enough for any taste.

Preparation time: 30 minutes   Cooking time: 5 minutes

2 medium onions,
  finely chopped
1/2 green pepper,
  finely chopped
2 cloves garlic, mashed
1/4 cup butter
2 cups soured cream
2 tsp. lemon juice

1/2 tsp. grated lemon rind
1-2 tsp. curry powder
1/4 tsp. chili powder
1/2 tsp. salt
1/2 tsp. freshly ground
  black pepper
1-1/2 lbs. cooked shrimp,
  peeled and deveined

Saute the onions, pepper and garlic in the butter until the onions are transparent. Stir in the soured cream, lemon juice, lemon rind, curry powder, chili powder, salt and pepper. When thoroughly blended, add shrimp. Heat through but do not allow to boil. Serve immediately with rice and condiments (chutney, coconut, chopped peanuts, crumbled bacon, etc.).

Barbequed Shrimp

Comments: These shrimp have a light, almost tropical flavor — lovely in the summer grilled over the barbeque.

Preparation time: 15 minutes   Cooking time: 4-5 minutes

1/2 tsp. garlic salt
1/2 tsp. ground ginger
1/4 tsp. salt
1/4 tsp. pepper

juice of 1 lime
1/2 cup vegetable oil
1/2 tsp. lime rind, grated
2 lbs. uncooked shrimp,
    peeled and deveined

Mix all ingredients together and marinate at least 3-4 hours, or overnight. Stir occasionally. Broil 4-5 minutes and serve with picks. Do not overcook or shrimp will be tough.

Seaford Shrimp

Comments: Mustard marinade takes this out of the ordinary.

Preparation time: 10 minutes   Cooking time: 30 minutes

2 cups cooked shrimp,   1/4 cup butter
   peeled and deveined   2 tbsp. flour
2 tbsp. lemon juice   1/2 tsp. salt
1/2 tsp. salt   1/4 tsp. pepper
1/2 tsp. paprika   1-1/2 cups light cream
1/2 tsp. dry mustard   3/4 cup buttered bread crumbs

Combine shrimp, lemon juice, salt, paprika and mustard in a bowl, and let marinate for 2 hours in the refrigerator stirring occasionally. In a saucepan, melt 1/4 cup butter, add 2 tbsp. flour and blend with a whisk. Add cream gradually, stirring constantly. Combine marinated shrimp and sauce in a shallow baking dish. Cover with crumbs and bake for 30 minutes at 350°.

Baked Sole

Comments: Freshness of ingredients is the key to this recipe.

Preparation time: 30 minutes   Cooking time: 20 minutes

1 tsp. salt	2 tbsp. melted butter
1/2 tsp. pepper	3 tbsp. onion, minced
1/8 tsp. mace	1/4 lb. fresh mushrooms, sliced
1/8 tsp. thyme, optional	2-3 tbsp. butter
2 lbs. fillet of sole	6 lemon wedges
1/2 cup dry vermouth	parsley for garnish
2 tbsp. lemon juice	

Coat fish in seasonings. Arrange the fish in a greased, shallow baking dish. Mix vermouth, lemon juice and melted butter. Pour over fish. Saute the onions and mushrooms in remaining 2-3 tbsp. of butter until the onions are transparent. Spread mixure evenly over the fish and bake for 20 minutes at 350°. Serve immediately.

Swordfish Steaks Chablis

SERVES 4

Comments: For variety, try this with bluefish.

Preparation time: 10 minutes   Cooking time: 20-25 minutes

4 swordfish steaks (2″ thick)	salt and freshly ground pepper
2 cups or more chablis	1/4-1/2 cup bread crumbs
4-6 tbsp. butter	2 lemons cut in wedges

Place swordfish steaks in dish just large enough to accommo-date them without crowding. Add wine. Allow to marinate for an hour, turning once. Remove steaks from the dish and place on broiler pan. Reserve the marinade for basting. Dot fish with 3 tbsp. of butter, season and broil for 10 minutes, basting once. Turn the fish, dot with remaining butter, sprinkle with crumbs and broil until brown and fish flakes easily, basting several times. Remove to a serving platter and garnish with lemon wedges.

Poultry and Game Birds

Chicken Breasts Alexis

SERVES 6

Comments: Complicated but well worth the effort!

Preparation time: 45 minutes   Cooking time: 1 and 1/2 hours

6 whole chicken breasts, boned,   1/2 tsp. rosemary
   but intact   1/3 cup almonds, sliced
1/2 cup dates, chopped   1 orange, sliced
1/4 cup onions, chopped   1/2 cup dates
1/2 cup butter   1-2 tbsp. flour
1 cup carrots, shredded   1-1/4 cups orange juice
2 cups herb flavoured   1/2 tsp. salt
   dry stuffing mix

Saute the onion in butter until transparent. Add the chopped dates, carrots, stuffing, rosemary and almonds. Toss gently. Season the insides of the chicken breasts with salt. Spoon dressing into the chicken breasts and sew the edges together. Place on a rack in a shallow baking pan and brush with melted butter. Bake at 300° for 1-1/2 hours, basting frequently. Garnish with orange slices. To prepare sauce: cut remaining dates into wedges. Mix flour with 1/4 cup orange juice and add the pan drippings and remaining orange juice. Add salt to taste. Heat until thickened, stirring constantly, and add dates. Arrange chicken breasts on platter and cover with sauce. Serve immediately.

Chicken Breasts in Wine

Comments: A successful dish for a large party.

Preparation time: 1 and 1/2 hours   Cooking time: 45 minutes to 1 hour

8 whole chicken breasts, boned and skinned	3/4 tsp. pepper
3/4 cup butter	2 bay leaves
1/2 cup cognac	1/8 tsp. thyme
3 lbs. fresh mushrooms	2-1/3 cups Sauterne
3 lbs. boiled onions, canned or prepared ahead	2 13-3/4 oz. cans chicken broth
1-1/2 tsp. salt	1/2 cup cornstarch
	2-1/2 cups heavy cream

Cut chicken breasts into halves. Brown in 1/2 cup butter. Divide chicken pieces between 2 heated 3 qt. casseroles. Warm cognac in a small saucepan, ignite and pour over chicken. The cognac will extinguish itself after a moment. Saute the onions and mushrooms in the remaining butter for about 5 minutes. Combine onions, mushrooms, salt, pepper, bay leaves, thyme, chicken broth and 2 cups of the Sauterne and pour over chicken. Cover and bake in a 325° oven for about 30 minutes or until chicken is tender. Remove bay leaves. Can be prepared ahead or frozen at this point. Make a paste of the remaining Sauterne and cornstarch, and gradually stir into the casseroles. Simmer over low heat and stir gently to thicken. Add heavy cream and simmer, covered, about 10 minutes. Serve in chafing dish or from casserole.

Chicken Chesapeake

Comments: An elegant and unusual buffet dish!

Preparation time: 30 minutes   Cooking time: 1 and 1/2 hours

3 whole chicken breasts,
   split, boned, and skinned
8 oz. smoked ham, thinly sliced
1 pint oysters or more
liquid from oysters
3 slices bacon, uncooked and halved
1 pkg. wild and long-grained
   rice, cooked
10-3/4 can cream of chicken soup

1/2 cup soured cream
1/2 cup medium cream
1/4 cup sherry
1 tsp. parsley flakes
1 generous pinch tarragon
salt and pepper to taste
Parmesan cheese
paprika

Put cooked wild rice mixture in bottom of a shallow baking dish. Cover with a layer of smoked ham. Place oysters on ham and cover with chicken breasts. Top each chicken breast with a piece of bacon. Blend all remaining ingredients, except cheese and paprika. Pour the sauce over the chicken. Sprinkle the top with Parmesan and paprika, and bake at 300° for 1 and 1/2 hours.

Note: May be prepared one day in advance and refrigerated.

Chicken Divan

Comments: If you're feeling adventurous, add a pinch of cayenne to the sauce.

Preparation time: 45 minutes   Cooking time: 30 minutes

2 lbs. fresh asparagus or
   broccoli, parboiled
4 cups cooked chicken,
   cut in large pieces
2 10-3/4 cans cream of chicken soup
1/2 cup mayonnaise
1/2 cup soured cream

1/2 tsp. curry powder or more
2 tsp. lemon juice
1-1/2 cups Cheddar cheese, grated
1 tbsp. butter, melted
paprika
slivered almonds

Combine the soup, mayonnaise, sour cream, curry powder and lemon juice. Mix until smooth. Place the asparagus or broccoli on the bottom of a greased baking dish. Cover with chicken, and then with the sauce. Sprinkle the top with the cheese, melted butter, paprika and slivered almonds. Bake at 350° for 30 minutes.

Chicken Nicoise

Comments: A variation on the famous Riviera salad theme.

Preparation time: 30 minutes   Cooking time: 40 minutes

chicken parts for 4 servings
2 tbsp. vegetable oil
2 tbsp. butter
16 oz. can tomatoes, chopped
    and seeded
1 onion, chopped

2 cloves garlic, minced
1/2 cup black olives, pitted
1 small bay leaf
1 tsp. thyme
fresh parsley, chopped
1/2 tsp. salt

Saute chicken in oil and butter. Remove chicken and saute onion and garlic in the same skillet. Place chicken in casserole with tomatoes, onion and garlic mixture, olives, bay leaf, thyme, salt and parsley. Bake at 350° for 40 minutes or until chicken is tender. Serve with rice.

Chicken Polonaise

Comments: Rich and delicious!

Preparation time: 15 minutes
(must allow at least 2 hours
 for chicken to soak in cream)

Cooking time: 8-10 minutes

4 whole chicken breasts, split,
  boned and skinned
1 tsp. salt
1/2 tsp. marjoram
1/4 tsp. pepper

1 cup medium cream or
  evaporated milk
2 eggs
3/4-1 cup butter or margarine
1/2 cup fine bread crumbs

Pound chicken pieces to 1/2" thickness. Season with salt, pepper and marjoram. Place in a shallow dish and add cream. Refrigerate for at least 2 hours, preferably overnight. Shortly before serving, beat the eggs and add 1/4 cup of the cream mixture from the chicken. Dip the chicken pieces in this mixture and roll in bread crumbs. Melt butter in a skillet, add chicken and cook, covered, over moderate heat, for 8-10 minutes, turning once. Serve immediately.

Chicken Rosé

Comments: Chicken is moist and flavourful.

Preparation time: 30 minutes   Cooking time: 55 minutes

4 whole chicken breasts,   3/4 cup rosé or dry white wine
   split and boned   1 medium onion, diced
11 tbsp. butter   1 cup fresh mushrooms, sliced
6-7 tbsp. flour   15 oz. can artichoke hearts, drained
1 cup chicken broth   or two pkg., frozen

Dust chicken with 3-4 tbs. flour. Place chicken skin-side down in a baking dish with 5 tbsp. of melted butter. Bake uncovered at 350° for 30 minutes. Make a roux of 3 tbs. butter and the remaining flour. Add broth and wine. Cook until smooth. Reduce oven temperature to 325° and turn chicken, removing some of the fat. Saute onions and mushrooms in 3 tbs. butter. Combine with artichokes and wine sauce. Pour over the chicken, cover, and bake for an additional 25 minutes. Serve immediately.

Chicken Veronique

SERVES 8

Comments: The secret is in the refrigeration.

Preparation time: 20 minutes   Cooking time: 1 hour
(allow for overnight refrigeration)

5 whole chicken breasts,
  boned and split
juice of 1/2 fresh lemon
1 medium onion, sliced
2 tsp. garlic salt
3 tbs. vegetable oil
1 pound seedless white grapes
1-1/2 cups dry white wine or
  chicken broth

4 tbsp. butter
2 tbsp. flour
2/3 cup light cream
1-1 1/2 cups Swiss cheese, grated
2 chicken bouillon cubes
Tabasco
2 egg yolks

Place 1 tsp. vegetable oil in a large skillet with garlic salt, 1 cup wine, and lemon juice. Add chicken breasts and onion slices and cover. Bring to a boil and simmer for 20 minutes. Remove chicken breasts from the broth and set aside. Reserve the broth, discarding the onion. Melt the butter and add 2 tbs. vegetable oil. Blend in the flour and the broth and cook, stirring constantly, until the sauce begins to thicken. Remove from heat and add cream, bouillon cubes and a dash of Tabasco. Return to heat and simmer briefly before setting aside. Remove the stems from the grapes, then cook them in 1 cup of water plus 1/2 cup of wine. Drain and set aside. To assemble: slice the chicken breasts and arrange them in a greased casserole. Sprinkle lightly with half of the cheese Cover with a layer of grapes. Add the egg yolks to the cream sauce, stir until well blended, and then pour over the chicken and grapes. Top with another layer of cheese and refrigerate overnight. Before serving, heat in a 350° oven for 20-25 minutes. Garnish with parsley.

Buffet Chicken Thermidor

Comments: A good way to use leftover chicken or turkey.

Preparation time: 40 minutes   Cooking time: 30 minutes

1 cup sharp Cheddar cheese, grated
10 oz. frozen peas, defrosted
2 cups cooked chicken, or turkey, diced
1 cup celery, chopped
5-oz. can water chestnuts, drained and thinly sliced
1/2 cup almonds, sliced

2 tbsp. pimiento, chopped
4 tbsp. white wine
1/2 tbsp. lemon juice
2 slices white bread, cubed
1/2 tsp. salt
3/4 cup milk
10 3/4 oz. can cream of chicken soup
2 tbsp. green pepper, chopped
1 tbsp. onion, minced

In a 2-quart casserole combine peas, chicken, celery, water chestnuts, almonds, green peppers, onion and pimiento. Sprinkle with the wine, lemon juice and salt. Toss gently. In a small saucepan, blend the milk and soup until smooth. Bring to a boil, stirring constantly. Pour sauce over casserole, and mix well. Cover with bread cubes and bake for 20 minutes at 350° until sauce is bubbly and the bread cubes are toasted. Sprinkle the top with the cheese and return to the oven for an additional 5 minutes. Serve immediately.

Country Captain Chicken

Comments: This had its origin in New England's clipper ship days.

Preparation time: 15 minutes   Cooking time: 1 hour

2 chickens, cut in serving pieces	1 large green pepper, chopped
1/4 cup flour	1 large clove garlic, crushed
2 tsp. salt	3 tsp. curry powder
1/2 tsp. pepper	1 can (1 lb.) tomatoes, quartered
3 tbsp. vegetable oil	1/2 cup raisins
1 large onion, chopped	

Combine flour, salt and pepper in a bag. Shake chicken, in the flour mixture, a few pieces at a time. Brown chicken in oil in a heavy skillet. Remove chicken to 200° oven. Add onion, green pepper, garlic, and curry powder to skillet with pan drippings. Saute until the onion is transparent. Add tomatoes, raisins and chicken. Simmer covered for 1 hour, or until chicken is tender. Arrange chicken on rice before serving, and spoon sauce over the top.

Oriental Roasted Chicken

Comments: A light and delicate flavour.

Preparation time: 15 minutes
(allow for overnight refrigeration)

Cooking time: 1 hour and 30 minutes

3-1/2 lb. chicken
1/2 cup soy sauce
1/3 cup vinegar

1-1/2 tbsp. dried onion
1/4 tsp. garlic powder

Combine soy sauce, vinegar, onion and garlic powder. Marinate chicken for 24 hours in this mixture. Reserve marinade. Roast, uncovered, for 1 and 1/2 hours at 325°, basting frequently with marinade.

The Boston Tea Party
from Ballou's Pictorial, 1856
Courtesy of the Bostonian Society, Old State House, Boston, Massachusetts

Oven Barbecued Chicken

Comments: Great for a crowd after a football game.

Preparation time: 30 minutes   Cooking time: 45 min. to 1 hour

chicken parts for 6 servings	**1 cup ketchup**
1/4 cup flour	**2/3 cup water**
1/4 cup vegetable oil	**2 tbsp. Worcestershire sauce**
3 tbsp. butter	**2 drops Tabasco**
1/2 cup onion, sliced	**1 tbsp. brown sugar**
1/2 cup green pepper, sliced	**1/4 tsp. salt**
1 cup mushrooms, sliced	**1/4 tsp. paprika**
	1/4 tsp. pepper

Rinse chicken pieces and dry well. Season flour with salt and pepper and coat chicken. Melt oil in a heavy skillet, add chicken and brown. Place in large casserole. Melt butter in a saucepan and add onion, green pepper and mushrooms. Cook until tender. Stir in remaining ingredients and bring to a boil. Pour the sauce over the chicken and bake the casserole for 45 minutes in a 350° oven.

Tailgate Chicken

Comments: Great for a picnic.

Preparation time: 30 minutes
(allow for overnight refrigeration)

Cooking time: 1 hour

5 or 6 whole chicken breasts,
  split and boned
2 cups soured cream
1 tbsp. Worcestershire sauce
1/2 tsp. Tabasco

1/8 tsp. garlic powder or
  1 clove, pressed
1 tsp. salt
1-1/2 tsp. paprika
1 cup bread crumbs or less

Coat chicken with a sauce made with all of the ingredients except bread crumbs. Place in a shallow dish and pour any remaining sauce over chicken. Cover tightly and refrigerate overnight. Coat each breast with bread crumbs, shape neatly and place one-layer deep in a shallow baking dish. Cover tightly and return to the refrigerator for at least 1-1/2 hours. Bake uncovered at 350° for 1 hour. Do not allow to brown, as the chicken breasts will dry out. Serve hot or cold.

Wild Duck with Fruit Dressing

Comments: Fabulous! Dressing can be used with other poultry or game birds.

Preparation time: 20 minutes   Cooking time: 1 and 1/2 hours

1 apple	12-oz. jar orange marmalade
1 large orange	4 wild ducks
1 medium onion	6 oz. undiluted frozen orange juice,
6 slices of stale white bread	thawed
3/4 cup white grapes	6 oz. brandy

Peel and dice apple and onion. Peel and section orange, leaving no membrane. Seed grapes and cut in half. Cut bread into small pieces. Combine all fruit with the marmalade and stuff into the cavity of the duck. Roast duck at 350° for 1 and 1/2 hours, basting frequently with a mixture of orange juice and brandy. Skin should be crisp. Serve immediately with the orange juice and brandy flavoured pan drippings.

Duckling a l'Orange

Comments: The duckling is moist but never greasy!

Preparation time: 5 minutes   Cooking time: 2 hours and 10 minutes

4-5 lb. duckling	6 whole black pepper corns
3 unpeeled oranges, quartered	1/2 cup butter, melted
2 cloves garlic, chopped	1/4 cup burgundy
1 tsp. salt	orange or lime marmalade

Fill duckling cavity with oranges, garlic, salt and pepper. Prick skin with fork. Roast for 30 minutes at 425°, then reduce heat to 375° and cook for an additional 40 minutes. Turn duck and continue roasting at 375° for 20 minutes; turn again and roast for 30 minutes longer at 375°. Baste frequently with a combination of melted butter and burgundy. Remove duckling from oven, coat the skin with orange marmalade, and return to the 375° oven to cook for an additional 10 minutes, or until marmalade is melted.

Pheasant Stuffed with Wild Rice

Comments: Pheasant is succulent and sweet — all white meat.

Preparation time: 1 hour   Cooking time: 1 hour

3 pheasants, whole	**1/4 cup butter, melted**
1/2 cup water	**1/2 cup port**

Make sure the pheasants have been thoroughly cleaned and all pin feathers removed. Brown pheasants in butter in a heavy skillet. Stuff with Wild Rice Dressing. Truss and brush with pan drippings. Place the pheasants breast-side down on a rack in a roasting pan. To the drippings in the pan, add water and port and baste frequently. Cover and bake at 350° for about 1 hour or until tender.

Wild Rice Dressing

3 cups cooked wild rice	1 cup mushrooms, chopped
1 egg, beaten	1/3 cup onion, chopped
1/4 lb. bulk sausage, cooked and drained	1 tbsp. butter
	pepper to taste

Saute the onion and mushrooms in the butter until the onion is transparent. Place the cooked wild rice in a large mixing bowl and add the beaten egg. Then add the sausage and the onions and mushrooms. Stuff the pheasants with the mixture.

Currant Jelly and Port Wine Sauce

1 tbsp. butter	8 oz. jar currant jelly
2 tbsp. port	

Melt the currant jelly in the top of a double boiler and add the other ingredients. Serve the sauce as an accompaniment to pheasant.

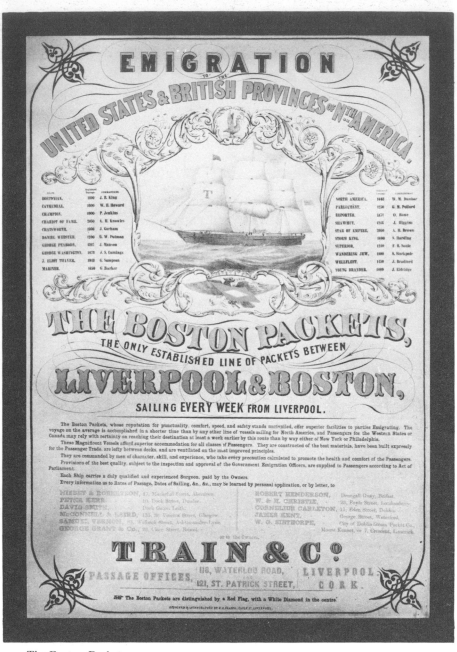

The Boston Packets
Broadside, circa 1850
Courtesy of the Bostonian Society, Old State House, Boston, Massachusetts

Meats

Beef Bourguignon

Comments: Superb results! Well worth the effort.

Preparation time: 45 minutes   Cooking time: 3 hours

1/2 lb. salt pork, diced
24 small white onions, peeled
4 lbs. lean beef, cut in 2" cubes
1 tbsp. flour
1/2 tsp. salt
1/4 tsp. pepper, freshly ground
1 clove garlic, minced
fresh parsley, chopped

1 bouquet garni (1 bay leaf,
  1 sprig thyme, 1/2 tsp.
  nutmeg, 1/2 tsp. marjoram,
  and a small bunch of parsley
  tied in cheesecloth)
2 cups red wine
2 cups fresh whole mushrooms
2 orange peels, sliced

Brown the salt pork in a dutch oven until crisp; remove and drain. Brown peeled onions in the drippings from the salt pork; remove the onions and brown the meat in the same pan. Sprinkle the salt pork with flour and return to the dutch oven. Season with salt and pepper; add garlic, orange peel and bouquet garni. Heat wine and pour over meat. Cover and place in a 275° oven. Bake for 3 hours, adding more wine as necessary. Saute the mushrooms in a little butter, until just transparent. Add the mushrooms and onions to the beef for the last 30 minutes of cooking time. Before serving, remove the orange peel and bouquet garni; thicken the gravy with 2 tbsp. of flour if too thin. Sprinkle with parsley.

Cape Malay Beef Stew

Comments: Easy to make, flavourful and fun to eat.

Preparation time: 1 hour   Cooking time: 3 hours plus

1 tbsp. butter	2-3 tsp. salt
1 tbsp. olive oil	1/2 tsp. chili powder
4 lbs. top round beef in	4 tbsp. curry powder
1" cubes	1 tbsp. sugar
3 medium onions, chopped	2 tbsp. cider vinegar
32 oz. can Italian tomatoes	

Combine butter and oil in a skillet and saute onions. Remove onions and brown meat in the same pan. Add tomatoes, salt, chili powder and sauted onions. Cover and cook over low heat for 30 minutes, stirring occasionally. Mix curry powder, sugar and vinegar until smooth and add to the meat. Cover and simmer for an additional 2-1/2 hours, adding water if necessary. The sauce will be thick. Serve with rice and any or all of the following condiments: minced raw onion, chopped cooked bacon, raisins, sliced banana, pine nuts, coconut.

Fast Beef Wellington

SERVES 6-8

Comments: A simple version of a favorite "masterpiece".

Preparation time: 15 minutes   Cooking time: 45-50 minutes

1 pkg. frozen puff pastry,
   thawed
2-1/2-3 lbs. fillet of beef
3 tbsp. cognac
salt and pepper

3 slices of bacon
8 oz. liver pate
1 egg beaten with
   1 tbsp. water

Preheat oven to 450°. Sprinkle the beef with cognac, salt and pepper, and lay bacon strips over top. Bake the beef for 17 minutes (rare) or 20-23 minutes (medium). Remove bacon and set aside to cool. Roll out pastry thinly on a well-floured surface. Spread pate on the center of the pastry, place fillet on top; fold up sides and seal ends. Place seam-side down on a baking sheet. Cut designs out of the excess dough and decorate the top. 35-40 minutes before serving time, brush the top of the crust with the egg mixture. Bake in a preheated 425° oven for 30 minutes. Serve with madeira sauce (add 3 tbsp. madeira to one can of beef gravy).

Sauer-bauer Beef

Comments: An interesting version of a traditional German favorite.

Preparation time: 40 minutes   Cooking time: 3-1/2 hours
(allow for 2-3 days refrigeration)

4-5 lbs. boneless beef roast	2 carrots, sliced
2 cups red wine vinegar	2 onions, quartered
4 cups water	1 tbsp. catsup
1 cup onion, sliced	1/2 cup gingersnaps, crushed
5 peppercorns	1/2 cup almonds, slivered
1 bay leaf	4 tbsp. butter
2 whole cloves	2 tbsp. sugar
1/4 tsp. thyme	1/2 cup red wine
parsley sprigs	1 cup currants
1/4 cup flour	

Combine vinegar, water and all spices except parsley; bring to a boil. Pour marinade over roast and cool. Add parsley and cover the container. Refrigerate for 2-3 days, turning several times. Strain marinade and reserve. Wipe meat dry and dredge in flour. Saute in 1/4 cup butter until brown on all sides. Add carrots, quartered onions, catsup and one cup marinade. Cover tightly and simmer for 2-1/2-3 hours or until tender. Remove meat to a warmed platter. Strain or puree the sauce; skim off fat and measure liquid. Add reserve marinade if necessary to make 2 cups. Add gingersnaps, sugar, wine and currants. Bring sauce to a boil and cook until thickened. Add almonds and pour sauce over sliced meat.

Rindsgoulash

Comments: This is an Austrian beef "Rinds" goulash with a fabulous flavour!

Preparation time: 30 minutes   Cooking time: 2 hours

1-1/2 lbs. beef, cubed	1/4 tsp. caraway seeds
1-1/2 lbs. onions, finely chopped	3 tbsp. tomato paste
1 tbsp. paprika	1 tbsp. lemon rind, grated
butter	1 clove garlic, crushed
salt	1/2 cup red wine
pinch marjoram	2 tbsp. water
coffee	2 tbsp. flour

Saute the onions in butter until transparent. Add paprika and water and stir. Add the beef and continue stirring until the meat is slightly browned, about 15 minutes. Add marjoram, tomato paste, lemon rind, garlic, and wine. Simmer, covered, very gently, adding water or coffee as necessary, until the beef is tender, about 1-1/2 hours. Add flour, water, salt and caraway to taste. Increase heat, stirring well for 15 minutes.

Note: Serve with nockerl, noodles, dumplings, or boiled potatoes. Flavour improves with each reheating.

Dolmathes

Comments: Greek stuffed grape leaves — delicious!

Preparation time: 1 and 1/2 hours   Cooking time: 1 hour

1 lb. ground lamb or beef
1/2 cup rice, uncooked
1 large onion, chopped
1/2 cup parsley, chopped
2 tsp. salt
1/4 tsp. pepper
2 tsp. fresh mint, chopped or
    1 tsp. dried

1/2 cup water
4 eggs
50 grape leaves
juice of 1 lemon
3 tbsp. butter, melted

Mix the first seven ingredients in a large bowl. Combine the water and 1 egg; beat, then add to the meat mixture. Wash grape leaves thoroughly. If canned or bottled leaves are used, rinse and boil in clear water for 5 minutes; drain well. Place about 1 tsp. of meat near the stem end of the leaf; roll slightly toward the tip of the leaf, until the two sides can be folded toward the center without tearing; continue rolling until the stuffed leaf is cigar-shaped, with no loose edges and no meat exposed. Place the stuffed leaves in layers in a large pan. Add the melted butter and enough water to barely cover the leaves. Weight the top of the leaves with a plate and simmer, covered, for 1 hour. Drain, reserving 2 cups of the liquid. At this point the dolmathes may be refrigerated until serving time. Just before serving, reheat the dolmathes and prepare an egg lemon sauce, as follows. Beat 3 eggs well in a double boiler, over boiling water. Pan should not be touching water. Add lemon juice slowly and stir until sauce begins to thicken. Gradually add 1 cup of warm liquid from the dolmathes, stirring constantly. Add more of the liquid if a thinner sauce is desired. Pour sauce over dolmathes and serve immediately.

Sauteed Frogs Legs

Comments: It's great fun to serve frogs legs at home and these are simple to prepare.

Preparation time: 2 minutes   Cooking time: 15 minutes

8 large frogs legs (thawed,   3/4 cup boiling chicken stock
   if previously frozen)   1-1/4 cups seasoned croutons,
2 tbsp. flour   crushed
salt and pepper   1 garlic clove, minced
9 tbsp. butter   1 tbsp. lemon juice

Put flour, salt and pepper in a plastic bag; add frogs legs and shake. Melt 6 tbsp. of the butter in a skillet and saute the minced garlic. Add the frogs legs and saute until they are browned. Add boiling stock and lemon juice; simmer for 10 minutes. Melt the remaining 3 tbsp. butter; add to the crushed croutons and toss. Roll the cooked frogs legs in the croutons and garnish with fresh lemon wedges and parsley. Serve immediately.

Ham with Noodles and Curry

Comments: An easy Sunday night supper, making good use of left-over ham.

Preparation time: 15 minutes   Cooking time: 10 minutes

1/2 cup butter, softened	1 cup light cream
1-1/2 tbsp. curry powder	noodles for 6
1/2 lb. ham in julienne strips	

Cook noodles according to package directions. Melt 1/4 cup butter and add curry and ham; cook until well heated about 4 minutes. Add noodles, then cream and remaining butter. Season with salt and pepper to taste. Serve immediately, or store in refrigerator and reheat in a covered casserole.

Lamb Tavern 1746 North Corner of Avery and Washington Streets
Courtesy of the Bostonian Society, Old State House, Boston, Massachusetts

125

Lamb Korma Curry

Comments: This is a true Indian curry. The creation of your own curry powder makes all the difference in the taste.

Preparation time: 10 minutes   Cooking time: 45-50 minutes

2 tbsp. ground coriander
1 tsp. cumin
1 tbsp. poppy seed
1 tsp. tumeric
4 cloves garlic
1" piece fresh ginger
1/4 tsp. cayenne
1 fresh or pickled green chili
3 tbsp. unsweetened coconut

1 tsp. paprika
6 cloves
1/4 tsp. ground cardamon
2 medium onions
2 lbs. lamb, cubed
3 tbsp. vegetable oil
2" stick cinnamon
1 tsp. salt
1 cup yogurt

Place all spices and 1 of the onions in a blender, and blend until a paste is formed. Chop the other onion and brown in the vegetable oil; add the spice paste and cinnamon stick and saute for 3 minutes. Add meat and saute for 5 minutes. Add salt and yogurt. Cover and simmer until the meat is tender, stirring occasionally. Add only enough water to prevent burning. The sauce should be thick. May be prepared early in the day and reheated.

Lamb with Lemon Sauce

Comments: Lettuce is a surprising and delicious addition.

Preparation time: 45 minutes   Cooking time: 2-1/2 hours

4 tbsp. olive oil	salt
4 tbsp. butter	freshly ground pepper
1 bunch scallions, chopped	white wine and chicken stock
1 head iceberg lettuce, shredded*	1 tsp. arrowroot or 3/4 tsp. cornstarch
2 large onions, chopped	juice of 1 lemon
3 lbs. lamb leg, cubed	rind of lemon, finely chopped
	3 egg yolks

May use Boston or Romaine lettuce or spinach.

Combine oil and butter in a large skillet. Saute scallions, lettuce, and onions until transparent. Add cubed lamb and cook, turning frequently, until the lamb changes colour but is not brown. Season with salt and pepper to taste. Cover meat with a combination of white wine and chicken stock and simmer gently for about 1-1/2 hours, or until lamb is tender. Combine arrowroot or cornstarch with lemon juice and rind, and mix thoroughly. Add the lemon mixture to the stew slowly, stirring constantly, and cook until the sauce begins to thicken. Remove from heat. Beat the egg yolks slightly, add a little sauce from the stew and blend. Slowly add the egg mixture to the stew, stirring carefully to prevent the sauce from separating. When the eggs have been blended, return the stew to low heat and cook until the sauce has thickened. *Do not boil.*

Marinated Leg of Lamb

Comments: An unusual marinade that can also be used for chops or shish-ke-bob.

Preparation time: 5 minutes   Cooking time: 25-40 minutes

6-8 lbs. leg of lamb, butterflied
  and boned
1 to 1-3/4 cup olive oil
3/4 to 1 cup wine vinegar
3 tbsp. soy sauce
1/3 cup pimiento, chopped
1/4 cup capers

2 tsp. salt
1/2 tsp. pepper
1/2 tsp. dill
1/2 tsp. tarragon
1/2 tsp. oregano
1 bay leaf, crushed
4 garlic cloves, mashed

Combine all ingredients (except lamb) and mix well. Place leg of lamb in a large casserole, add marinade and refrigerate for at least 6 hours. Turn occasionally. Cook over a barbecue or under broiler for 5 minutes on the first side, 10 minutes on the second side, then an additional 5-7 minutes on each side or until lamb is pink in the middle.

Variations: A simpler marinade can be made using 1 cup soy sauce, 1 cup dark molasses, 1 cup brown sugar and 1 cup cider vinegar. The taste is distinctively different, and the marinade accentuates the flavour of the lamb without overpowering it.

For a more traditional Greek marinade, combine 1/2 cup Dijon mustard, 2 tbsp. soy sauce, 2 tsp. ground ginger, 1 tsp. thyme, 1 mashed clove of garlic and 2 tbsp. olive oil. Combine the first 5 ingredients; beat the oil into the mixture gradually, using a whisk. Spread on the lamb and refrigerate for at least 6 hours.

Pork Chops Tamari

Comments: The Tamari sauce is an unusual flavour with pork.

Preparation time: 15 minutes   Cooking time: 30-40 minutes

4 pork chops (1" thick)
1 tsp. Dijon mustard
1/3 cup Tamari sauce*
juice of 1/3 lemon
1/3 cup Madeira

1 large onion, sliced in
  1/2" slices
chicken stock (1 cup for gravy)
1 tbsp. cornstarch
2 tsp. parsley, chopped

Tamari sauce is fermented soy sauce — available in natural food stores. Soy sauce can be substituted.

Combine mustard, Tamari, lemon juice and Madeira, and marinate the pork chops for 1-2 hours, turning the chops occasionally. Broil chops in the marinade about 20 minutes, basting with the marinade when necessary. Add chicken stock to the marinade if it begins to evaporate. During the last 10 minutes of cooking, add the onion slices and turn once while cooking. When the chops are done, remove them to a platter and keep warm. Dissolve the cornstarch in one cup of chicken stock and add to the pan drippings. Stir over low heat until the gravy begins to thicken. Add more chicken stock or water if gravy becomes too thick; it should be the consistency of fresh cream. Add the parsley to the gravy and serve over the chops and onions.

Meats   129

Harvest Pork Chops

SERVES 4-6

Comments: An Alsatian-type casserole that's as easy to prepare
as it is delicious.

Preparation time: 10 minutes   Cooking time: 40-50 minutes

6 loin pork chops (1/2″ thick)
16-oz. can sauerkraut,
    undrained
1 cup applesauce

1/4 cup onion, finely chopped
2 tbsp. brown sugar
1 tsp. caraway seed
1/4-1/2 cup dry white wine

Trim the excess fat from the chops and brown chops slowly on
both sides. Combine the remaining ingredients and pour over the
chops, adjusting the amount of wine to taste. Season with salt
and freshly ground pepper. Cover and simmer until chops are
tender.

Pork Loin in Red Wine

Comments: Simple and delicious.

Preparation time: 15 minutes   Cooking time: 2 hours and 20 minutes

3-4 lbs. pork loin	salt
1/4 cup parsley, chopped	pepper
1/4 cup onion, chopped	sage
1 bay leaf	nutmeg
2 cups red wine	1 clove garlic, crushed
1 cup canned beef consomme	6-8 new potatoes, peeled

Rub the roast with salt, pepper, sage and nutmeg. Place the roast and the garlic in a skillet and brown the roast on all sides. Place roast in a roasting pan; add the wine, consomme, onions, bay leaf, parsley and new potatoes. Bake for 2 hours and 20 minutes in a 350°, turning the meat occasionally.

Indonesian Skewered Pork

Comments: Unusual flavour — lovely for a summer barbecue.

Preparation time: 30 minutes   Cooking time: 20-30 minutes
(allow for overnight refrigeration)

1/4 cup pine nuts	3 tbsp. fresh lemon juice
2 tbsp. coriander (freshly ground, if possible)	1/4 cup soy sauce
	1 tbsp. brown sugar
1 clove garlic	1-1/2 lbs. pork, cubed
1/2 small onion	2 cucumbers or zucchini
1/4 tsp. freshly ground pepper	4 tomatoes
dash cayenne	1/4 cup butter, melted
3/4 tsp. salt	

Blend the first ten ingredients together. Leave pork in marinade for 3 hours or more, overnight is best. Peel cucumber or zucchini and quarter lengthwise; remove seeds and cut pulp into 1" chunks. Quarter tomatoes; halve each quarter. Thread skewers alternating with meat and vegetables. Cook slowly over charcoal for 20-30 minutes, basting with butter as needed.

Veal Supreme

Comments: Spectacular results—minimum effort!

Preparation time: 15 minutes   Cooking time: 1 1/2 hours

3 lbs. veal stew meat	1 pint soured cream
1 lb. fresh mushrooms, sliced	2 10-3/4 oz. cans cream of
2 medium onions, sliced	mushroom soup
2-3 tbsp. butter	1/4 cup sherry

Brown veal in the butter and remove to a large casserole. Brown mushrooms and onions in same pan. Place veal, mushrooms and onions in the casserole. Combine the soured cream, soup and sherry and pour over the meat. Bake, uncovered, for 1-1/2 hours at 350°.

Meats

Veal Veronique

Comments: Elegant presentation using an economy cut.

Preparation time: 30 minutes   Cooking time: 1-1/2 hours

2 tbsp. vegetable oil	1/2 cup chicken broth
2-1/2 lbs. veal stew meat	3/4 cup white wine
1/2 cup onion, chopped	1/2 cup water
1/2 clove garlic, mashed	1 carrot, pared and sliced
1/4 cup flour	1 celery rib, cut in diagonal slices
2 tsp. salt	2 tbsp. fresh parsley
1/8 tsp. pepper	1 egg yolk
1 tsp. dill	1/4 cup heavy cream
1/4 tsp. nutmeg	2 cups white seedless grapes

Brown veal in oil. Remove meat from pan. Cook onion and garlic in the same oil until tender. Return meat to the pan, and sprinkle with the flour, dill, salt, pepper and nutmeg. Add the chicken broth, wine, water, celery, carrots, and parsley, and mix well. Cover and simmer for 1-1/2 hours or until veal is tender. May be refrigerated at this point. Just before serving reheat the veal in the skillet. Blend egg yolk and cream together until smooth. Add a small amount of the warm sauce from the veal and stir. Add egg and cream mixture to the veal and mix well. Gently stir in the grapes and heat just until grapes are warm. Do not boil. Pour into a serving dish and garnish with parsley.

Vegetables

Barley Casserole

Comments: Easy and different.

Preparation time: 10 minutes   Cooking time: 1 hour

2 tbsp. butter	1/4 tsp. pepper
1 small onion, sliced	1 cup boiling water
2 cups pearl barley	1 lb. mushrooms, sliced
3 10-3/4 oz. cans beef broth	

Saute the onions in butter until transparent. Add the barley and continue cooking until the barley is lightly browned. Turn into a buttered 1-1/2 quart casserole. Just before baking, bring the broth to a boil; add the broth, pepper, water and mushrooms to the barley and stir gently. Bake, covered, for 1 hour or until the barley is tender. Add additional water or broth if necessary. Serve immediately after baking.

Broccoli Almondine

Comments: A saucy guise for broccoli.

Preparation time: 25 minutes   Cooking time: 30 minutes

1 lb. fresh broccoli or	1 tsp. salt
2 pkgs. frozen	1/4 tsp. pepper
2 tbsp. butter	1/4 cup almonds, chopped
2 tbsp. flour	4 slices crisp bacon, crumbled
2 cups milk	1/2 cup buttered bread crumbs
3/4 cup Cheddar cheese, grated	

Cook broccoli until tender. Drain and place in a buttered casserole. Melt the butter; stir in flour to form a roux. Add milk gradually, stirring until smooth; add cheese and stir over low heat until the cheese is melted. Season with salt and pepper. Sprinkle the broccoli with almonds, then pour the cheese sauce over all. Sprinkle the top with crumbs and bacon; bake at 350° for 30 minutes.

Broccoli Supreme

Comments: Substantial do-ahead party fare.

Preparation time: 20 minutes   Cooking time: 30-35 minutes

1-1/2 lbs. fresh broccoli	1 tbsp. onion, grated
10-3/4 oz. can cream of chicken soup	1/4 tsp. salt
1 tbsp. flour	1/8 tsp. pepper
1/2 cup soured cream	3/4 cup herb-seasoned
1/4 cup carrots, grated	stuffing mix
	2 tbsp. butter, melted

Remove outer leaves of broccoli and tough parts of stalks; discard. Slice the broccoli stems into 1″ pieces and cook in boiling salted water for 5-8 minutes; add broccoli flowerets and cook for an additional 5 minutes. Drain. Combine the soup, flour, soured cream, carrots, onion, salt and pepper. Stir in broccoli. Place the mixture in a 2-quart casserole. Combine the stuffing and melted butter; sprinkle around the edges of the casserole. Bake at 350° for 30-35 minutes. Serve immediately.

Carrots Cointreau

Comments: A nice addition to a Thanksgiving menu.

Preparation time: 10 minutes   Cooking time: 20 minutes

1 lb. young carrots	1/2 tsp. nutmeg
6 tbsp. butter, melted	1 oz. Cointreau or orange liqueur
1 tbsp. sugar	salt and pepper to taste

Cook carrots in lightly salted water until tender. Drain, reserving liquid; puree the carrots in a blender with about 1/4 to 1/2 cup of the cooking liquid. Add the butter, sugar and nutmeg to the puree. Heat the puree, season to taste with salt and pepper and stir in the Cointreau. Serve immediately.

Carrot Souffle

SERVES 8

Comments: Delicious — never falls!

Preparation time: 30 minutes   Cooking time: 45 minutes

2 cups carrots, cooked and mashed	1/4 tsp. cinnamon
	1 tbsp. flour
1/2 cup butter, softened	1 tsp. baking powder
1 cup sugar	1 tsp. salt
3 eggs	1 cup milk

Beat all ingredients together, combining until smooth. Pour into a 2-quart casserole dish and bake at 350° for 45 minutes.

Copenhagen Carrots

SERVES 8

Comments: An unusual way to prepare carrots.

Preparation   time: 15 minutes   Cooking time: 15 minutes

2 lbs. carrots, peeled and sliced   1/4 cup butter
3 stalks celery, chopped   1/2 large onion, chopped
   (including leaves)   1/3 cup sugar of less
1/2 tbsp. dill   3/4 cup white wine or sherry

Combine all ingredients in a large saucepan. Cover and bring to a boil; simmer until the carrots are tender, about 15 minutes.

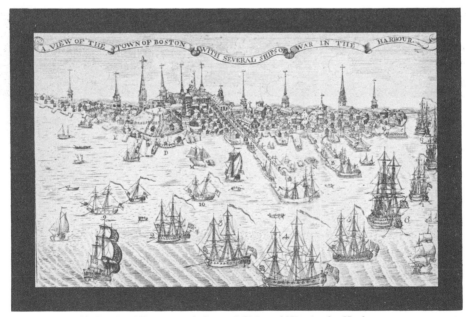

View of the Town of Boston with Several Ships of War in the Harbor
by Paul Revere II, 1773
Courtesy of the Museum of Fine Arts, Boston, Massachusetts

Bubble and Squeak

SERVES 6

Comments: A talkative casserole! Delicious with corned beef, ham or hot dogs.

Preparation time: 45 minutes   Cooking time: 25 minutes

1 lb. cabbage, chopped (outer leaves and core removed)
1 lb. potatoes, peeled and quartered

1/4 cup butter plus 2 tbsp.
1 cup Cheddar cheese, grated
1/2 cup onions, minced
2 tbsp. chives, chopped

Cook chopped cabbage in boiling salted water for 10 minutes or until tender. Drain; rinse under cold water and drain again. Boil the potatoes separately in salted water until tender. Drain potatoes, chop and place in a large bowl with the cabbage. Saute the onion and chives in 1/4 cup butter until soft but not browned; add to the potato-cabbage mixutre and toss to combine. Transfer the vegetables to a buttered 1-1/2 quart shallow casserole. Dot with 2 tbsp. butter and sprinkle the top with the cheese. Bake at 350° for 20 minutes or until the cheese is melted and the vegetables are heated through. Brown under the broiler if desired.

Note: Excellent reheated.

Hot Curried Cabbage

SERVES 4-6

Comments: Worth even a Russian cabbage queue!

Preparation time: 45 minutes   Cooking time: 20 minutes

10-3/4 oz. can beef broth	4 tbsp. butter
1 cup water	2 tbsp. flour
1 bay leaf	1 tbsp. curry powder
3 whole cloves	1 tsp. salt
1/2 tsp. salt	black pepper
3-3-1/2 lbs. cabbage, shredded	1-1/2 cups soured cream
1 medium onion, chopped	1/4 cup bread crumbs
1 clove garlic, crushed	

Simmer broth, water, bay leaf, cloves and 1/2 tsp. salt in kettle for 5 minutes. Remove bay leaf and cloves; add cabbage to the broth. Cover and simmer for 10 minutes, stirring occasionally. Drain, reserving 1/2 cup of the broth. Saute onion and garlic in butter until onion is transparent; blend in flour, curry powder, 1 tsp. salt and pepper. Gradually add the soured cream and broth. Cook over low heat, stirring constantly, until sauce simmers and thickens. Combine sauce and cabbage and place in a casserole. Sprinkle with crumbs and bake at 425° for 15-20 minutes or until crumbs are browned.

Eggplant Casserole

Comments: A delightful medley of flavours.

Preparation time: 15 minutes   Cooking time: 45 minutes

1 large eggplant, peeled and
   diced
1/4 cup butter
1/2 cup cream
1 cup soft bread crumbs
3/4 cup Cheddar cheese, grated
3 tbsp. tomato paste
   or catsup

1 tsp. salt
1 small onion, minced
dash white pepper
few dashes liquid Maggi
   seasoning
2 eggs, beaten

Put the eggplant in a covered saucepan with 1/4 cup water, and simmer until the eggplant is soft. Mash with a potato masher without removing from pan. Continue cooking, uncovered, until most of the excess moisture has cooked away. Remove from heat and add all ingredients except eggs. Cool mixture and blend in eggs. Put in a casserole dish and bake at 350° for 45 minutes, or until the top has browned slightly.

Note: Can be prepared early in the day and stored, unbaked, in the refrigerator.

Green Beans Beau Monde

SERVES 6

Comments: A nice accompaniment to fish or beef.

Preparation time: 20 minutes   Cooking time: 30 minutes

2 cans (1 lb.) cut green beans   1-1/2 cups Cheddar cheese, grated
4 tbsp. butter   1-1/2 tsp. Beau Monde seasoning
3 tbsp. flour   1/2 cup bread crumbs
1/4 tsp. salt   3/4 cup milk

Drain beans, reserving 3/4 cup of the liquid. Melt 3 tbsp. of the butter and stir in flour to make a roux. Gradually add the milk and green bean liquid, stirring constantly until smooth. Add cheese and cook over low heat until the cheese is melted. Add Beau Monde seasoning, salt and beans. Pour into a buttered baking dish, sprinkle with bread crumbs and dot with the remaining butter. Bake at 350° for 30 minutes.

Mushroom Casserole

SERVES 6

Comments: Rich and tasty. Serve as a side dish with poultry
or red meat.

Preparation time: 15 minutes   Cooking time: 30 minutes

2 cups bread cubes   butter
Parmesan cheese, grated   marjoram or thyme
1 cup light cream or milk   1 tbsp. onion, chopped
1 lb. fresh mushrooms

Remove caps from mushrooms and place in a layer in a buttered
casserole dish. Chop the mushroom stems; saute in butter with
the onions. Combine the stems and onions with the bread cubes,
and place over the mushroom caps in the casserole. Sprinkle
with grated cheese and marjoram or thyme; pour the cream
over all. Bake for 30 minutes in a 350° oven. Serve immediately.

Mushrooms Gruyère

Comments: Rich, fattening, irresistible.

Preparation time: 10 minutes   Cooking time: 30 minutes

1 lbs. fresh mushrooms, sliced	1 cup medium cream
4 tbsp. butter	6 oz. Gruyere cheese

Saute mushrooms in melted butter until golden but not crispy. Pour off liquid. Pour cream over mushrooms and let simmer for about ten minutes or until liquid is considerably reduced. Remove contents to a shallow casserole. Shred cheese over top of mushroom mixture. Bake for 20 minutes or until bubbly at 350°.

Mushrooms Koussevitzski

Comments: Based on a Polish favorite!

Preparation time: 15 minutes   Cooking time: 15 minutes

3/4 lb. fresh mushrooms	1 tbsp. flour
1 tbsp. lemon juice	2 tbsp. Parmesan cheese
1 tbsp. onion, finely minced	1 cup heavy cream
3 tbsp. butter	2 egg yolks, lightly beaten
1/4 tsp. salt	2 tbsp. fine bread crumbs
1/8 tsp. pepper	sherry to taste

Butter a casserole or 4 individual ramekins. Slice the mushrooms and sprinkle with the lemon juice. Simmer the mushrooms in a tightly covered suacepan with the onion and 2 tbsp. of the butter; season with salt and pepper. Remove mushrooms and add the flour to the juice left in the pan. Add Parmesan cheese. Cook, stirring constantly; combine with the mushrooms and place in casserole. Mix the heavy cream and egg yolks together, and add sherry to taste. Pour over the mushrooms. Sprinkle with bread crumbs and dot with the remaining 1 tbsp. of butter. Bake at 425° for about 10 minutes or until the top is golden brown.

Heavenly Onions

Comments: A great accompaniment for beef or pork.

Preparation time: 15 minutes   Cooking time: 40 minutes

2 large Bermuda onions	1/2 cup milk
2 tbsp. butter	1 tbsp. soy sauce
1/2 lb. Muenster or Swiss	1 cup buttered bread crumbs
cheese, sliced	1/4 tsp. pepper
10-3/4 oz. can cream of mushroom soup	
or cream of chicken soup	

Peel and slice onions; separate into rings and saute in butter with the pepper until transparent. Place the onions in a shallow baking pan and cover with the cheese. In a separate bowl combine the soup, milk and soy sauce. Pour the mixture over the onions and cheese. Top with buttered bread crumbs and bake for 40 minutes at 350°.

Potatoes Chantilly

Comments: Similar to a souffle.

Preparation time: 20 minutes   Cooking time: 15 minutes

> **4 cups mashed potatoes, seasoned with butter,**
> **salt and pepper**
> **1/2 cup cream, whipped**
> **1/3 cup Cheddar cheese, grated**

Place the mashed potatoes in a buttered baking dish. Top with a layer of whipped cream and cover with grated cheese. Bake at 425° until cheese is melted and the top is golden brown and bubbly.

North Shore Potatoes

Comments: A much requested recipe.

Preparation time: 30 minutes
(allow for overnight refrigeration)

Cooking time: 45 minutes

6 medium potatoes, boiled in skins	dash freshly ground pepper
2 cups soured cream	1/2 medium onion, minced
1-2 tsp. salt	6 tbsp. butter
	2 cups Cheddar cheese, shredded

Store cooked potatoes in the refrigerator for 24 hours. Melt 4 tbsp. of the butter with the cheese in a double boiler. Add the soured cream, salt, pepper and onions and stir until well blended. Remove from heat. Peel the potatoes; grate them and stir into the cheese mixture. Place the mixture in a casserole. Dot with remaining butter and bake at 350° for 45 minutes. Serve immediately.

Note: Can be assembled early in the day and refrigerated until cooking time. Potatoes must be cooked 24 hours in advance.

Spinach Surprise

Comments: Allow for second helpings!

Preparation time: 15 minutes   Cooking time: 30 minutes

3 10 oz. pkgs. frozen
  chopped spinach
1/2 cup butter
1 cup creamed cheese
2/3 tbsp. lemon juice

salt and pepper
buttered bread crumbs
15-oz. can artichoke hearts,
  or 10-oz. pkg. frozen artichoke
  hearts

Cook spinach according to directions on package. Drain well. Melt butter and cheese over low heat, stirring until smooth; add lemon juice. Pour the cheese sauce over the spinach and mix thoroughly. Add salt and pepper to taste. Place the artichoke hearts, cut in thirds, in the bottom of a buttered 1-1/2 quart casserole. Cover the artichoke hearts with the spinach mixture; top with buttered bread crumbs and bake at 350° for 30 minutes.

Arabian Squash Casserole

SERVES 6-8

Comments: Delicious, especially with barbecued beef or fowl.

Preparation time: 30 minutes   Cooking time: 1 hour

3 lbs. summer squash	5 eggs, beaten
1 tbsp. salt	1 cup bread crumbs
1-1/2 cups Cheddar cheese grated	1/2 tsp. pepper
1 cup cottage cheese	4 tbsp. butter, melted

Peel and grate the squash; mix with the salt and let stand for 20 minutes. Press out liquid. Combine the squash with all remaining ingredients except the butter, and pour into a buttered 3-quart casserole dish. Pour the melted butter over the top, and bake at 350° for 1 hour or until brown on top and firm. Serve immediately, or keep warm in the oven for a maximum of 20 minutes.

Squandered Squash

Comments: Do not be frightened when squash is shrivelled and wizened! It is sweet and delicious.

Preparation time: 10 minutes   Cooking time: 1 hour

medium, plump zucchini or summer squash
butter
black pepper
oregano with zucchini

Rinse squash well. Slice in half lengthwise, and place skin side down in shallow baking pan. Dot generously with butter and sprinkle with pepper. Oregano is optional, but adds a nice flavour to the zucchini. Bake at 400° for 1 hour.

Tarragon Tomatoes

Comments: A colourful vegetable which can be used as a garnish for a buffet.

Preparation time: 3 minutes   Cooking time: 8-10 minutes

24 cherry tomatoes	1 tsp. sugar
4 tbsp. butter, melted	1 tsp. tarragon

Place tomatoes in a baking dish with other ingredients. Bake at 350° for 8-10 minutes, shaking the pan occasionally so the tomatoes turn in the butter. Serve immediately.

Paul Revere's Ride
from Harper's Weekly, 1867
Courtesy of the Bostonian Society, Old State House, Boston, Massachusetts

Tourlou Tava

Comments: Greek Ratatouille; freshness of ingredients is the key.

Preparation time: 1 hour   Cooking time: 2 hours

2 lbs. fresh string beans	2 10 oz. pkgs. frozen okra (thawed)
4-6 medium zucchini, sliced	4 cloves garlic
2 large onions,	1 cup parsley, chopped
quartered and sliced	2 lb. can Italian tomatoes, chopped
1/4 cup dill, chopped	salt and pepper to taste
1/2 cup olive oil	

Combine vegetables and herbs, except zucchini and okra, in a large casserole. Cover and bake at 450° for about 10 minutes, or until liquid starts to simmer; reduce heat to 350° and bake for 1 hour. Add the zucchini and okra and bake for an additional hour, or until the vegetables are all tender.

Note: It is always tastier when made the day before serving, and can be kept in the refrigerator for up to a week or frozen.

Wild Rice and Mushrooms

SERVES 10

Comments: Delicious with game birds.

Preparation time: 15 minutes   Cooking time: 1-1/2 hours

8 oz. wild rice	2 stalks celery, chopped
1/2 cup butter	1/2 lb. fresh mushrooms, sliced
3 large onions, chopped	1 tbsp. salt
1 green pepper, chopped	1 tbsp. wine vinegar

Rinse rice under cold water until water runs clear. Cook the rice according to package directions, adding 1 tbsp. wine vinegar to the water. Saute the onions in the butter until transparent; add the green peppers, celery and mushrooms, and cook until light brown. Combine the rice and vegetables and place in a casserole. Cover and bake for 30 minutes at 350°.

Zucchini Cheese Custard

Comments: An elegant addition to any meal.

Preparation time: 15 minutes   Cooking time: 35 minutes

4 small zucchini	2/3 cup light cream or milk
2 medium onions	1/4 tsp. nutmeg
1/4 cup butter, melted	3 eggs, beaten
1-1/2 cups sharp Cheddar cheese, grated	salt and pepper to taste

Slice zucchini into 2″ rounds. Peel onions and slice thinly. Saute the onions and zucchini in butter until light golden brown. Do not allow the zucchini to get soft. Spoon the zucchini and onions into a shallow casserole. Combine the eggs, cream, nutmeg and half of the cheese; pour the sauce over the vegetables. Sprinkle the rest of the cheese over the top and season with salt and pepper. Place the casserole in a pan of hot water in a 350° oven and bake for 35 minutes, or until the custard is set. Serve immediately.

Zucchini Pancakes

Comments: Terrific for brunch.

Preparation time: 20 minutes   Cooking time: 15-20 minutes

1/3 cup Bisquick
1/4 cup Parmesan cheese,
   grated
2 eggs, beaten

6 tbsp. butter
1/2 tsp. salt
1/8 tsp. pepper
2 medium zucchini

Shred unpared zucchini; press out excess liquid. Combine the eggs, Bisquick, cheese, salt and pepper; fold in the zucchini. Melt 2 tbsp. of the butter in a large skillet and cook the first four pancakes for 2-3 minutes on each side. Repeat with second and third batches. Serve immediately.

Zucchini Puff

Comments: An elegant way to serve squash.

Preparation time: 25 minutes   Cooking time: 20 minutes

3 large or 6 small
   zucchini or summer squash
2 tbsp. butter, melted
1/2 tsp. pepper
1 tsp. salt

1-1/2 cups milk
1 tbsp. flour
2/3 cup Gruyere cheese, grated
4 eggs, well beaten

Peel and dice squash; place in a saucepan with the butter, salt and pepper. Cover and cook over low heat until the squash is soft. Beat together eggs, milk, and flour. Add squash to egg mixture. Blend well, and pour into a buttered 2-quart casserole. Sprinkle with cheese and bake at 400° for 20 minutes.

Cottage Zucchini

SERVES 6

Comments: Perfect use for "over-grown" squash.

Preparation time: 30 minutes   Cooking time: 30 minutes

1 large zucchini	2 tbsp. parsley, chopped
2 eggs, well beaten	2 tbsp. onion, chopped
1-1/2 cups sharp Cheddar cheese, grated	salt and pepper to taste cracker crumbs
1/2 cup cottage cheese	butter

Boil the zucchini whole until barely tender. Split lengthwise and remove seeds. Combine all other ingredients except cracker crumbs and butter; fill the zucchini halves with the mixture. Sprinkle with cracker crumbs and dot with butter. Bake at 350° for 25-35 minutes. Cook longer if the zucchini is very large, or has been refrigerated.

Note: Can be assembled early in the day and refrigerated until baking time.

Salads and Salad Dressings

Molded Cranberry Salad

Comments: A colourful side-dish, especially good with poultry.

Preparation time: 10-15 minutes

8 oz. can crushed pineapple	1-1/2 cups boiling water
1 envelope unflavoured gelatin	2 cups soured cream
3 oz. pkg. raspberry gelatin	1 lb. can cranberry sauce

Drain pineapple, reserving liquid. Add the unflavoured gelatin to the pineapple liquid and let stand for 5 minutes. Add the raspberry gelatin to the boiling water; blend in the pineapple gel. Stir until dissolved; cool in a separate bowl, combine the soured cream, pineapple and cranberry sauce; mix thoroughly. Stir into the gelatin mixutre. Pour into a 2-quart mold which has been lightly oiled. Chill until firm.

Cucumber Lime Cream Mold

Comments: Marvelous on a hot day.

Preparation time: 25 minutes   Cooking time: 10 minutes
(allow for refrigeration)

9 oz. lime-flavoured gelatin
1-1/2 tsp. salt
2-2/3 cups boiling water
2 tbsp. vinegar
cherry tomatoes

1-1/2 pints soured cream,
2 cups cucumbers, pared, seeded
  and finely chopped
2/3 cup scallions, chopped or
  Bermuda onions
cucumber slices

Dissolve gelatin in boiling water in a large bowl. Stir in the vinegar and chill until slightly thickened. Beat in soured cream; fold in cucumbers, onion, and salt. Pour into a 2-qt. mold which has been lightly oiled and chill for 4 hours, or until firm. Unmold onto lettuce leaves and garnish with slices of cucumber and cherry tomatoes.

Marinated Cucumbers

Comments: Marvelous when cukes overflow the garden!

Preparation time: 15 minutes   Cooking time: 5 minutes
(allow for overnight refrigeration)

1 cup cider vinegar	1 medium red onion,
1 cup sugar	thinly sliced
1 tbsp. salt	4 cups cucumbers,
1 tbsp. celery seed	peeled and thinly sliced

Combine all ingredients, except onion and cucumbers, and bring to a boil. Add onions and cucumbers. Fill quart jar with the mixture. Refrigerate overnight before serving. The marinade may be "recycled" by adding more cucumbers. Keeps indefinitely in the refrigerator.

Fruit and Chicken Salad

Comments: Good for a summer luncheon!

Preparation time: 15 minutes   Cooking time: 20 minutes

3 cups chicken,
   cooked and diced
1 cup celery, diced
1 cup Mandarins orange sections*

1 cup pineapple chunks
mayonnaise
2 tbsp. vegetable oil
2 tbsp. orange juice
2 tbsp. vinegar

Seedless white grapes may be substituted

Combine chicken, celery, orange sections and pineapple chunks. Blend the oil, orange juice, vinegar and toss with the chicken mixture. Chill one hour. Drain and add enough mayonnaise to bind. Serve on lettuce leaves.

Holiday Fruit Mold

SERVES 8-12

Comments: Refreshingly different. Many other fruits can be substituted with equally pleasing results.

Preparation time: 30 minutes
(allow for refrigeration)

2 cans jellied cranberry sauce
2 envelopes unflavoured
  gelatin
1/2 cup cold water
1/8 tsp. cinnamon
1/4 tsp. salt
grated rind of 1 orange

juice of 1 orange
3/4 cup walnuts or
  pecans, chopped
3/4 cup apples, peeled and diced
1/2 cup celery, chopped
1/4 cup red wine

Soften the gelatin in the water; heat until dissolved. Break up the cranberry sauce and add the gelatin. Stir until smooth. Chill the mixture until almost set; stir in the remaining ingredients and mix well. Pour into a lightly oiled 2-qt. mold and refrigerate until set.

Salads and Salad Dressings

Italian Garden Salad

Comments: Delightfully addictive!

Preparation time: 15 minutes
(allow for overnight refrigeration)

Cooking time: 10 minutes

2 cups cauliflower flowerets
2 carrots, cut in strips
2 stalks celery, in 1″ pieces
1 green pepper, cut in strips
1 small jar salad olives
  (5-6 oz.), drained
1 8-1/2-oz. can artichoke
  hearts, drained and cut in
  halves

1 cup fresh mushroom caps,
  stems removed
3/4 cup wine vinegar
1/4 cup olive oil
2 tbsp. sugar
1 tsp. salt
1/2 tsp. oregano
1/4 tsp. freshly ground pepper
1/4 cup water

Combine all ingredients in one layer in a large skillet and stir. Bring to a boil, stirring occasionally. Reduce heat and simmer, covered, for 5 minutes. Remove from heat, cool and refrigerate for at least 24 hours before serving.

Potato Salad de Luxe

Comments: Lovely rich flavour.

Preparation time: 20 minutes   Cooking time: 20-30 minutes

8 medium new potatoes
1 can bouillon
1 medium red onion, finely
  chopped
12 cherry tomatoes
4 hard-boiled eggs, diced

chopped parsley
salt and pepper to taste
1 cup mayonnaise,
  preferably homemade
1 4-oz. can artichoke hearts,
  drained and sliced

Boil the potatoes in their jackets until tender. Drain, peel and slice. Marinate the potatoes in the bouillon for 1 hour. Combine the chopped onion with the whole cherry tomatoes, sliced artichoke hearts, diced eggs, and a sprinkling of chopped parsley. Add salt and pepper to taste. Drain the potatoes from the marinade and gently fold into the vegetable-egg mixture; blend in mayonnaise. Chill.

German Potato Salad

Comments: Marvelous for a buffet, especially with ham.

Preparation time: 25 minutes   Cooking time: 5 minutes

1 quart boiled potatoes, diced	1 tbsp. mustard
1 onion, diced	4 tbsp. sugar
1 egg	6 slices bacon
1/4 cup cider vinegar	1 tsp. salt
1/4 cup water	1/4 tsp. pepper

Fry bacon until crisp. Remove from pan, reserving drippings. Combine the egg, sugar, mustard, salt and pepper and beat well. Add the vinegar and water to the egg mixture, adding extra vinegar to taste; combine the mixture with the bacon drippings. Cook until the sauce thickens; combine the sauce, potatoes, onions and crumbled bacon. Place the mixture in a casserole and keep warm in the oven until serving time.

Salade de Cressons

Comments: Try this instead of a Waldorf!

Preparation time: 10 minutes

2 bunches watercress
1/2 cup olive oil
1/4 cup wine vinegar
2 tbsp. heavy cream
1/2 tsp. sugar
salt to taste
freshly ground pepper

1 bunch scallions, sliced (white part only) or one small onion
1/2 lb. fresh mushrooms, thinly sliced
chervil sprigs
chopped chives
2 apples, peeled and diced

Combine the oil, vinegar, cream, sugar, salt and pepper. Marinate the mushrooms and onions in this mixture for 1 hour. Just before serving, place watercress on each plate. Add the apple into the dressing and spoon onto cress. Top with a sprinkling of fresh herbs.

Note: If fresh herbs are not available, substitute dried herbs and add to dressing with apple.

Snappy Vegetable Medley

Comments: An outstanding combination!

Preparation time: 5-10 minutes
(allow for overnight refrigeration)

1/3 cup brown sugar	1 lb. canned corn, drained
2/3 cup cider vinegar	1 large onion, diced
2/3 cup vegetable oil	2 cucumbers, peeled, seeded
salt and pepper to taste	and sliced
1 lb. canned green beans,	2 tomatoes, peeled and chopped
drained	

Combine brown sugar, vinegar and oil. Add salt and pepper to taste. Add the vegetables to the dressing and refrigerate in a covered container overnight. Will keep up to 2 weeks in the refrigerator.

South Market Street, Boston
by Winslow Homer, circa 1860
Courtesy of the Bostonian Society, Old State House, Boston, Massachusetts

South Pacific Salad

Comments: Exotic!

Preparation time: 1 hour   Cooking time: 20 minutes

3 pineapples	6" watermelon wedge
3/4 cup sugar	3 bananas, rolled in chopped walnuts
1 pint strawberries	1 melon: honeydew or cantaloupe

Cut pineapples through the crown into halves; hollow out the fruit to form shells, using a grapefruit knife. Remove the core of the pineapple and cut fruit into 1/2 inch cubes. Sprinkle with 3/4 cup of sugar and return to shells. Wash and hull the strawberries, reserving 12 unhulled berries for garnish. Cut melon into halves; remove seeds and scoop out balls with a melon scoop. Prepare one cup watermelon balls using the same method. Just before serving, peel bananas, roll in coarsely chopped nuts and slice each banana into sixths with a french fluted cutter. Place pineapple halves on a large shiny leaf on luncheon plate. Then arrange the strawberries, melon balls and banana slices around each shell. Top with the reserved strawberries. Serve with South Pacific Salad Dressing.

South Pacific Salad Dressing

Comments: Though this is intended as the companion to South Pacific Salad, it is equally good on any fruit salad.

Preparation time: 5 minutes   Cooking time: 15-20 minutes

1 tbsp. cornstarch
2 tbsp. water
1/3 cup lemon juice
2/3 cup orange juice

1 tbsp. Maraschino liquid (optional)
1 cup sugar
2 eggs, beaten
1 cup heavy cream, whipped

Mix the cornstarch and water; add the fruit juices, sugar and eggs. Cook in a double boiler, stirring constantly, until thick. Cool slightly and refrigerate. Just before serving, fold in the whipped cream. Makes 2 cups.

Creamy Spinach Salad

Comments: Especially good with beef.

Preparation time: 15 minutes

1 lb. raw spinach, rinsed and drained	2 tbsp. red or white wine vinegar
1 medium onion, thinly sliced	2/3 cup mayonnaise
2-3 hard-boiled eggs, sliced	2 tbsp. cream or milk
2 tbsp. sugar	1 tsp. salt

Just before serving, combine sugar, vinegar, mayonnaise, cream and salt. Toss with the spinach and onion rings. Garnish with egg slices.

Spinach and Bacon Salad

Comments: Terrific when cold winds blow.

Preparation time: 15-20 minutes   Cooking time: 5-10 minutes

1 lb. raw spinach	1-2 tbsp. wine vinegar
4-5 slices bacon	1 tsp. dry mustard
5-6 chopped scallions, greens included	2 tbsp. brown sugar

Rinse and tear the spinach into bite-sized pieces. Saute the bacon until it is crisp. Remove from pan, drain, reserving fat. Crumble bacon and return to the fat in the pan. Add the remaining ingredients except spinach. Heat until the sugar is dissolved, and pour the warm dressing over the spinach. Serve immediately.

Note: Prepare dressing early in the day and reheat just before serving.

Tomato Aspic

Comments: An easy and reliable recipe.

Preparation time: 15 minutes
(allow for refrigeration)

Cooking time: 5 minutes

1 large can tomatoes (2 lb., 3-oz.)
6-oz. pkg. strawberry gelatin
1 tbsp. horseradish

1/2 cup celery, finely chopped
1/2 cup green pepper,
    finely chopped

Place tomatoes (do not drain) in blender and blend for 1 minute. Transfer to a large saucepan and boil for 2 minutes. Add the strawberry gelatin and stir until dissolved. Put the horseradish in a bowl; add the tomato mixture, celery and peppers. Mix well and pour into a lightly oiled 2-qt. mold. Refrigerate for several hours before unmolding.

Anchovy Salad Dressing

Comments: A treat for anchovy lovers!

Preparation time: 5 minutes

2-3 anchovy fillets, chopped   coarsely-ground pepper
1/2 tsp. Dijon mustard   1/4 cup olive oil
1 tbsp. wine vinegar

Mash the anchovies and combine with the mustard, vinegar and pepper to taste. Add the olive oil and beat dressing until well blended. Serve at room temperature.

Aunt Effie's Salad Dressing

YIELD: APPROX. 1 CUP

Comments: Nice, tangy flavour.

Preparation time: 5 minutes

1/3 cup olive oil	1/2 tsp. dry mustard
1/3 cup wine vinegar	1/4 tsp. paprika
1/3 cup ketchup	salt and pepper to taste
1/4 cup sugar	

Combine all ingredients and mix thoroughly. Will keep well for up to 1 week under refrigeration.

Creamy Salad Dressing

YIELD: 1-1/2 CUPS

Comments: A very good and easy homemade dressing.

Preparation time: 5 minutes

1/3 cup red wine vinegar	1 tbsp. parsley, chopped
1 cup olive oil	1 tsp. tarragon, crushed
1 egg	2 tbsp. Parmesan cheese, grated
1 clove garlic, crushed	

Combine all ingredients and blend well.

Feta Cheese Dressing

YIELD: 1-1/2 CUPS

Comments: A change from Roquefort.

Preparation time: 5 minutes

1 cup olive oil
1/4 cup lemon juice
salt and pepper to taste

2 cloves garlic, crushed
oregano to taste
1/4 lb. feta cheese, crumbled

Combine the oil and lemon juice. Add salt, pepper, garlic and oregano. Mix well. Crumble feta cheese into the mixture and refrigerate overnight. Serve at room temperature.

Poppy Seed Dressing

YIELD: 1 CUP.

Comments: Great on fruit salads.

Preparation time: 10 minutes

3/4 cup sugar
1 tsp. dry mustard
1 tsp. salt

1/3 cup vinegar
1 cup vegetable oil
1-1/2 tbsp. poppy seeds

Mix the sugar, mustard, salt and vinegar in a blender. Gradually add the oil, forming a creamy consistency. Add the poppy seeds and blend a few moments longer. Refrigerate until serving time.

Sweet and Super Dressing

YIELD: 1-1/2 CUPS

Comments: From a popular Back Bay tea room.

Preparation time: 10 minutes

1/2 cup sugar	1/2 cup onion, minced
1 tsp. dry mustard	1 cup vegetable oil
1 tsp. salt	celery seed to taste
1/3 cup cider vinegar	

Combine the first four ingredients thoroughly. Add onions, then gradually add the oil. Season to taste with celery seed. Add more vinegar if the dressing is too sweet. Serve over raw spinach, tossed with bacon crisps, mushrooms and onion slices, or over your favorite salad greens.

Breads

Apple Muffins

Comments: A seasonal specialty — cider gives the magic touch.

Preparation time: 15 minutes   Cooking time: 45 minutes

1/3 cup butter, softened	1-1/2 tsp. baking soda
1 cup sugar plus	1 tsp. cinnamon plus
1 egg	1/2 cup sweet cider
1-1/2 cups flour	1 medium Cortland apple
1/2 tsp. salt	

Cream sugar and butter. Stir in egg and cider. Sift dry ingredients together and add to the batter. Peel and core the apple; cut into thin wedges. Roll the wedges in cinnamon and sugar; stir into the muffin batter. Fill paper muffin cups or buttered muffin tin 2/3 full. Bake at 375° for 45 minutes.

Blueberry Muffins

Comments: Especially good in summer when berries are fresh.

Preparation time: 5-10 minutes   Cooking time: 20-25 minutes

1 egg	1/2 cup sugar
1/2 cup milk	2 tsp. baking powder
1/4 cup vegetable oil	1/2 tsp. salt
1-1/2 cups flour	1 cup berries*

*Blueberries or raspberries.

Beat the egg, then add the milk and oil. Blend in the dry ingredients and stir until just moistened. The batter will be slightly lumpy. Gently fold in the berries. Fill paper muffin cups or buttered muffin tin 2/3 full and bake at 400° for 20-25 minutes.

Cranberry Nut Loaf

YIELD: 1 LOAF

Comments: Keep cranberries in the freezer to do this at a moment's notice.

Preparation time: 15 minutes   Cooking time: 50-60 minutes

2 cups sifted flour
1-1/2 tsp. baking powder
1/2 tsp. baking soda
1 egg
1/4 cup shortening
1 tsp. salt

1" x 2" piece orange rind
1 cup sugar
3/4 cup crange juice
1/2 cup nuts
1 cup cranberries

Sift flour, baking powder and soda into a large bowl. Put the egg, shortening, salt, orange rind, sugar, orange juice into a blender. Cover and blend at high speed until the rind is grated finely. Add nuts and cranberries and blend only until chopped. Combine the cranberry mixture with the dry ingredients and stir until the dry ingredients are moistened. Spoon into a buttered and floured loaf pan. Bake at 350° for 50-60 minutes.

Dilly Bread

YIELD: 1 LOAF

Comments: A real treat for herb lovers.

Preparation time: 30 minutes
Rising time: 2-1/2 — 3 hours

Cooking time: 35-45 minutes

1 pkg. dry yeast
1/4 cup warm water
1 cup creamed cottage cheese
   at room temperature
2 tbsp. sugar
2 tbsp. onion, minced
1 tbsp. butter

2 tsp. dill
1 tsp. salt
1/4 tsp. baking soda
1 egg, beaten
2-1/4-2-1/2 cups flour

Soften the yeast in the warm water, then combine the yeast with all of the ingredients except flour. Mix until thoroughly blended. Gradually add the flour until a stiff dough is formed. Knead for 7-8 minutes. Place in a buttered bowl, turning once to butter both sides of the dough. Let rise until doubled in bulk, or about 1-1/2-2 hours. Punch down and shape the dough into a loaf; place in a buttered loaf pan and set aside to rise again until doubled, about 1 hour. Bake at 350° for 35-45 minutes.

Breads

185

Holiday Stollen

YIELD: 4 LOAVES

Comments: A lovely holiday bread. Great for gifts!

Preparation time: 1 hour   Cooking time: 30 minutes
Rising time: 4 hours

2 cups milk	1/4 cup citron
1 pkg. dry yeast	1/2 tsp. lemon rind
7-1/2 cups flour	1/2 cup blanched almonds
3 eggs, beaten	juice of 1/2 lemon
1 cup sugar	1/4 tsp. nutmeg
1 tsp. salt	1/2 tsp. cinnamon
1 cup shortening, melted	1/2 cup candied fruit
2-1/2 cups raisins	and peels

Sprinkle yeast over 1/4 cup lukewarm water; let stand for 5 minutes, then stir to dissolve. Scald the milk and stir in the yeast. Add 1-1/2 cups of the flour and place dough in a warm place for 15-20 minutes until it bubbles. Blend eggs, sugar, salt, and melted shortening. Dredge the fruit in a little flour and blend into the mixture; then add the lemon rind, almonds and lemon juice. Sift together the remaining flour, nutmeg and cinnamon. Add both the flour mixture and the fruit mixture to the yeast dough, and blend to form a stiff dough. Turn the dough out on a floured board and knead until smooth (about 10 minutes) adding more flour if necessary. Place dough in a buttered bowl approximately twice the size of the ball of dough. Cover with a damp cloth and let rise in a warm place until the dough has doubled in bulk (about 2-3 hours). When doubled in bulk, punch down. Knead again gently for 2-3 minutes. Shape the dough into small loaves, place in four buttered loaf pans, and let rise again until doubled in bulk (about 1 hour). Bake for 30 minutes at 375°. Frost with powdered sugar icing.

Irish Bread

YIELD: 1 LOAF

Comments: A combination of Boston and Gaelic receipts!

Preparation time: 15 minutes   Cooking time: 1 hour

2-1/2 cups flour
2 tsp. baking powder
1 tsp. salt
1/2 tsp. baking soda
1/4 cup butter
1/2 cup sugar
1 egg, beaten

1-1/2 cups buttermilk (or
  1-1/2 cups milk + 1-1/2 tbsp.
  vinegar)
1 cup raisins
1/2 cup currants
1 tbsp. caraway seeds

Sift the flour, baking powder, salt, soda together. Set aside. Cream the butter and sugar. Add the egg and buttermilk, and blend well. Add the liquid mixture to the flour mixture, and mix until the dry ingredients are well moistened. Fold in the raisins, currants and caraway. Pour into a buttered 1-1/2-quart casserole, brush the top with melted butter, and sprinkle with a little sugar. Bake at 375° for 30 minutes, then reduce the heat to 325° and bake for an additional 30 minutes. Test the bread to see that it is done before removing from the oven by tapping the loaf near the center. It is done if it sounds hollow.

Note: For easier toasting, use a loaf pan.

Letitia's Lemon Loaf

YIELD: 1 LOAF

Comments: Incredibly easy with a marvelously tangy lemon flavour.

Preparation time: 20 minutes   Cooking time: 60 minutes

6 tbs. crisco	1/8 tsp. ground cloves
1-1/4 cups sugar	1-1/2 tsp. baking powder
2 eggs, beaten	1/3 tsp. salt
1-1/2 cups flour plus 1 tbs.	rind of 1 lemon, grated
1/2 cup milk	juice of 1 lemon
1/4 tsp. orange extract	1/4 cup sugar
1/8 tsp. lemon extract	

Cream shortening and sugar. Add beaten eggs, extracts and grated rind. Blend. Sift in flour, baking powder, salt and cloves. Mix well. Beat for a minute or two. Add milk and mix thoroughly. Pour into a buttered and floured loaf pan. Bake at 350° for 60 minutes. While the bread is still warm, combine lemon juice and 1/4 cup sugar and pour over the top of the bread. Let stand in pan until absorbed.

Note: Even better when wrapped in foil and refrigerated overnight!

Monkey Bread

Comments: A grand buffet bread — it's already buttered!

Preparation time 45 minutes   Cooking time 45-55 minutes

Rising time: 4 hours

2 cups milk	1 tsp. baking soda
1/3 cup sugar	1 tsp. baking powder
1/2 cup shortening	2-1/2 tsp. salt
1/4 cup warm water	1/2 cup butter, melted
1 pkg. dry yeast	
5 cups sifted flour	

Scald milk and mix in sugar and shortening. Let cool to luke-warm temperature. Dissolve yeast in warm water; Let rest for 5 minutes. Add to milk mixture. Beat in 3 cups flour by hand. Cover with cloth and let rise for 2 hours in a warm place. Then work in remaining flour which has been sifted with baking soda, powder and salt. Cover and let rise for another hour in a warm place. Turn the dough out on a well-floured surface and spread out with hands. Pinch off pieces of dough and make 1-1/2-2" diameter balls. Dip each ball in melted butter and arrange side by side in a Bundt or tube pan making several layers. Cover pan and let rise again until double in size about 45 minutes to an hour. Bake at 350° for 45-55 minutes.

Orange Nut Bread

YIELD: 1 LOAF

Comments: A brunch bread from the sunny south!

Preparation time: 15 minutes   Cooking time: 50-60 minutes

1/2 cup butter, softened	1 tsp. orange rind, grated
1 cup sugar	1/4 cup orange juice,
2 eggs	freshly squeezed
1-1/4 cups flour	1/2 cup milk
1 tsp. baking powder	1/4 cup sugar
1/2 tsp. salt	1/2 cup pecans, finely chopped

All ingredients should be at room temperature. Cream butter and one cup sugar. Beat in the eggs, one at a time. Sift together the flour, baking powder and salt. Alternately add the flour mixture and milk to the butter mixture. Mix in the orange rind and nuts. Pour into a buttered loaf pan, preferably metal and bake at 350° for 50-60 minutes. Prepare a glaze by combining the orange juice and 1/4 cup sugar; blend until sugar is dissolved. When the cake comes out of the oven, poke holes in the top and pour the glaze over all. Let stand until cool before removing the cake from the pan.

Portuguese Sweet Bread

Comments: This recipe originated in a Nantucket guest house.

Preparation time: 30 minutes   Cooking time: 35-45 minutes
Rising time: 4-5 hours

6 to 7 cups flour   6 eggs, beaten
2 pkgs. dry yeast   1-2/3 cup evaporated milk
1 tsp. salt   4 tbsp. butter
1-1/4 cup sugar

Mix 2 cups of the flour, sugar, salt and dry yeast in a large mix
ing bowl. Warm the milk and butter; add to the flour mixture,
and beat with electric mixer at low speed until blended. Add
the eggs and continue beating; add 1 cup flour and beat at
medium speed for an additional 2 minutes. Stir in remaining
flour until stiff dough forms. Turn dough onto a well-floured
surface and knead for 8-10 minutes. Place in a buttered bowl,
turning once to butter both sides. Cover and let rise in a warm
place until doubled in bulk, 2-3 hours. Punch down and let
dough rest for 5 minutes. Divide into 4 equal parts; shape into
loaves and place in four buttered loaf pans. Let rise for 2 hours.
Bake at 350° for 35-45 minutes, covering the top of the loaf
with foil after the first 20 minutes. For a round loaf, bake
dough in oven-proof mixing bowls. Remove loaves from pans
and cool on a wire rack.

Pumpkin Bread

Comments: With canned pumpkin on the shelf, this can be whipped up in minutes.

Preparation time: 5-10 minutes   Cooking time: 1 hour

1-1/2 cups sugar	1/2 tsp. cinnamon
1-2/3 cups flour	1/2 cup vegetable oil
1/4 tsp. baking powder	1/2 cup water
1 tsp. baking soda	1 cup pumpkin, mashed
3/4 tsp. salt	2 eggs
1/2 tsp. ground cloves	1/2 cup nuts, optional
1/2 tsp. nutmeg	

Sift dry ingredients together. Stir in remaining ingredients. Pour the batter into a buttered and floured loaf pan and bake for 1 hour at 350°.

Sour Cream Coffee Cake

Comments: At holiday time, add candied fruit to the batter.

Preparation time: 20 minutes   Cooking time: 45 minutes

1/2 cup butter, softened	pinch salt
1 cup sugar	1 tsp. vanilla
2 eggs	1/2 cup nuts, chopped
1 cup soured cream	1 tsp. cinnamon
2 cups cake flour	1/4 cup packed brown sugar
1 tsp. baking powder	1 apple, diced or raisins
1 tsp. baking soda	

Cream butter and sugar; add eggs and vanilla. Sift the dry ingredients together and add to the butter mixture alternately with the soured cream. Pour half of the batter into a buttered and floured tube pan. Combine the chopped nuts, cinnamon, brown sugar and apple. Sprinkle half of the mixture over the first layer of batter in the pan. Pour the remaining batter into the pan and top with the remaining nut mixture. Bake at 350° for 45 minutes.

Strawberry Banana Bread

Comments: The strawberries are a perfect complement to the
bananas.

Preparation time: 10-15 minutes   Cooking time: 60-65 minutes

1-1/2 cups sifted flour	2 eggs, slightly beaten
2/3 cup sugar	1/2 cup mashed strawberries
2 tsp. baking powder	(about 1 cup whole berries)
3/4 cup quick-cooking oats	1/2 cup mashed bananas
1/2 tsp. salt	(about 1 medium banana)
1/3 cup vegetable oil	

Sift the flour, sugar, baking powder and salt in a mixing bowl.
Stir in the oats, then add the remaining ingredients. Stir gently
until the dry ingredients are moistened. Pour into a buttered
and floured loaf pan and bake for 60-65 minutes in a 350° oven.
Turn out of the pan and cool on a wire rack. Refrigerate overnight tightly wrapped before slicing.

Zucchini Bread

Comments: A great summertime treat!

Preparation time: 15 minutes   Cooking time: 1 hour

3 eggs
1-1/2 cups sugar
1 cup vegetable oil
2 cups zucchini,
   peeled and grated
1 tbsp. vanilla
3 cups flour

1 tsp. salt
1 tsp. baking soda
1/4 tsp. baking powder
1 tbsp. cinnamon
1 cup walnuts, chopped

Beat eggs in a large mixing bowl; add sugar, oil, zucchini and vanilla. Sift together dry ingredients and add to egg and zucchini mixture. Add walnuts. Pour batter into two buttered and floured loaf pans. Bake at 350° for 1 hour.

BOSTON,
Plymouth & Sandwich
MAIL STAGE,

CONTINUES TO RUN AS FOLLOWS:

LEAVES Boston every Tuesday, Thursday, and Saturday mornings at 5 o'clock, breakfast at Leonard's, Scituate; dine at Bradford's, Plymouth; and arrive in Sandwich the same evening. Leaves Sandwich every Monday, Wednesday and Friday mornings; breakfast at Bradford's, Plymouth; dine at Leonard's, Scituate, and arrive in Boston the same evening.

Passing through Dorchester, Quincy, Wyemouth, Hingham, Scituate, Hanover, Pembroke, Duxbury, Kingston, Plymouth to Sandwich. *Fare*, from Boston to Scituate, 1 doll. 25 cts. From Boston to Plymouth, 2 dolls. 50 cts. From Boston to Sandwich, 3 dolls. 63 cts.

N. B. Extra Carriages can be obtained of the proprietor's, at Boston and Plymouth, at short notice.—
☞STAGE BOOKS kept at Boyden's Market-square, Boston, and at Fessendon's, Plymouth.

LEONARD & WOODWARD.

BOSTON, *November* 24, 1810.

Boston Plymouth and Sandwich Mail Coach
Broadside, 1810
Courtesy of the Bostonian Society, Old State House, Boston, Massachusetts

Desserts

Apple Cake

Comments: A moist apple "pound cake". Particularly good
with tea.

Preparation time: 30 minutes   Cooking time: 1 hour

3 cups Macintosh apples, cored,
   peeled and diced
3 cups flour, sifted
2 eggs
2 cups sugar
1-1/2 cups vegetable oil

1 tsp. vanilla
1 tsp. baking soda
1/2 tsp. salt
1 tsp. cinnamon
1 cup walnuts or pecans, chopped

Dredge apples and nuts thoroughly with 1 cup of the flour. Beat
eggs and sugar together; add shortening and vanilla, then dry
ingredients. Add apple and nut mixture. Mix until apples and
nuts are evenly distributed through the batter. The batter will
be thick. Bake in a buttered Bundt pan or two loaf pans for 1
hour at 375°. Dust with powdered sugar while warm.

Creamy Cheese Cake

Comments: Simple enough even for a novice baker.

Preparation time: 30 minutes   Cooking time: 45 minutes
(allow for refrigeration)

6 oz. package graham crackers	1 cup sugar
4 tbsp. butter, melted	1-3/4 tsp. vanilla
2 tbsp. sugar	1 pint soured cream
1/4 tsp. cinnamon	1 lb. cream cheese, softened
	3 eggs, separated

Crush graham crackers and mix with the butter, 2 tbsp. sugar and cinnamon. Press into bottom and sides of a 9″ spring form pan. Reserve a small amount of the crumbs to decorate top. Combine the cream cheese, 1/2 cup of the sugar, egg yolks and 3/4 tsp. vanilla and mix until smooth. Beat the egg whites until stiff and fold into the cream cheese mixture. Spread the batter evenly in the crust and bake for 20-30 minutes at 375°. Cool for 1 hour. Mix the soured cream, remaining sugar and remaining vanilla. Spread the soured cream mixture over the top of the cooled cake. Sprinkle with the reserved graham cracker crumbs, and bake at 475° for 10-15 minutes. Cool and refrigerate.

Note: Can also serve topped with fresh fruit or fruited pie filling.

Coconut Pound Cake

Comments: An old-fashioned pound cake.

Preparation time: 20 minutes   Cooking time: 1-1/2 hours

1 lb. butter, softened	1/2 cup water
3 cups sugar	2 tsp. coconut flavouring, vanilla
2 cups flour	may be substituted
6 eggs	7 oz. flaked coconut

Cream the butter and 2 cups of the sugar with an electric mixer. Add 1 cup of flour; then add the eggs, one at a time. Mix the remaining flour with the coconut before blending into the batter. Add 1 tsp. coconut flavouring. Bake in a buttered and floured tube pan at 325° for 1-1/2 hours. Make a glaze by boiling the remaining 1 cup sugar, water and coconut flavouring for 8-10 minutes. Brush glaze over the cake while it is still warm.

Note: May be frozen. Glaze after thawing.

Ghiaradelli Chocolate Cake

Comments: For variety, substitute soured cream for soured
milk.

Preparation time: 10-15 minutes   Cooking time: 40 minutes

4 squares unsweetened chocolate	1-1/2 tsp. baking soda
1 cup boiling water	1-1/4 tsp. salt
2 cups sugar	1/2 cup soured milk*
1/4 cup butter	2 eggs
2 cups flour	1 tsp. vanilla

Melt chocolate in the top of a double boiler; add water and
stir. Cream butter and sugar and add to chocolate. Sift dry
ingredients. Add to the chocolate mixture alternately with the
soured milk. Beat eggs lightly and add to the mixture along
with the vanilla. The mixture will be thin. Pour into a buttered
and floured 9" x 13" pan and bake at 325° for 45 minutes.

*1-1/2 tsps. vinegar will sour 1/2 cup milk.

Kastanientorte

Comments: Chestnut cake: a pure delight for chestnut lovers!

Preparation time: 1 hour   Cooking time: 40 minutes

1 lb. fresh chestnuts,
or 3 cups canned chestnuts
5 eggs, separated
1 cup sugar
2 tsp. vanilla
3/4 cup blanched almonds

1/2 tsp. salt
1-1/2 tsp. baking powder
2 tbsp. milk
3 cups heavy cream
fruit preserves

Prepare the chestnuts the day before, as the shelling process is time-consuming. Wash the chestnuts and make a long slit in both sides of each shell. Boil for 1 hour and drain. Before the chestnuts are cool, shell them. When ready to make the cake, grind the chestnuts in a food grinder; set aside. Grind almonds and set aside. Beat the egg yolks in a large bowl with an electric mixer until light in colour and fairly thick (about 5 minutes). Add the vanilla and sugar, 1 tbsp. at a time and continue beating for another 15 minutes. Combine the almonds with the salt and baking powder and add to the egg mixture along with the chestnuts and milk. Blend well. Beat the egg whites until stiff and carefully fold into the chestnut mixture. Put equal amounts of batter into each of two 8" spring-form pans. Bake for 35-40 minutes at 350°. Let the cake stand for 5 minutes after removing it from the oven, then remove the rims from the pans. Continue cooling and then remove the bottoms of the pans from the layers. Store the layers in a cool place, wrapped in foil. About 2 hours before serving, whip the cream until a stiff, spreading consistency. Do not over-beat. Fill the first layer with fruit preserves (seedless raspberry is best), then cover with a layer of whipped cream. Place the second layer on top and cover the whole cake with the remaining whipped cream. Chill until serving time.

Note: To use 9" spring-form pans, increase batter recipe one and a half times. The cream measurement remains the same.

East View of Faneuil Hall Market
by Andrews and Bowen 1827
Courtesy of the Bostonian Society, Old State House, Boston, Massachusetts

Chocolate Pudding Cake

Comments: An old fashioned rich pudding cake that is a real treat!

Preparation time: 20 minutes   Cooking time: 40 minutes

1-1/4 cups sugar	1/2 cup milk
1 cup flour	1/2 tsp. vanilla
2 tsp. baking powder	1/2 cup brown sugar
1/8 tsp. salt	4 tbsp. unsweetened cocoa
1 oz. unsweetened chocolate	1 cup cold water
2 tbsp. butter	

Sift 3/4 cup of the sugar together with the flour, baking powder and salt. Melt chocolate and butter. Add to the flour mixture, and then add the milk and vanilla. Pour into a buttered 9″ x 9″ baking pan. Combine the remaining 1/2 cup sugar with the brown sugar and cocoa. Sprinkle evenly over the top of the pan and cover with the water. Bake for 40 minutes at 325°. Serve hot or cold, topped with sweetened whipped cream.

Mystery Torte

Comments: A special New England favorite.

Preparation time: 30 minutes   Cooking time: 30 minutes
(allow for overnight refrigeration)

16 Ritz crackers	1 tsp. vanilla
2/3 cup walnuts or pecans	1 cup heavy cream, sweetened
3 egg whites	and whipped
1 cup sugar	1 square unsweetened chocolate,
1/2 tsp. baking powder	grated

Chop crackers and nuts finely in blender. Beat egg whites until very stiff. Gradually add sugar and baking powder then the cracker mixture and the vanilla. Spread in a well-buttered 8" pie pan and bake for 30 minutes at 350°. Refrigerate overnight. Just before serving, top with the whipped cream and sprinkle with grated chocolate.

Orange Ring Cake

Comments: An unusual and rich cake.

Preparation time: 30 minutes   Cooking time: 1 hour

1 cup butter	3 egg whites
1-3/4 cups sugar	3 egg yolks
grated rind of 1 orange	1 cup soured cream
2 cups sifted cake flour	dash salt
or 1-3/4 cups all-purpose	juice of 2 oranges
1 tsp. baking powder	juice of 1 lemon
1 tsp. baking soda	

Cream butter and 1 cup of the sugar. Add the egg yolks, soured cream and rind, beating until light and fluffy. Sift flour, soda and baking powder and add to the butter mixture. Beat the egg whites until stiff but not dry and fold into the batter. Pour into a buttered and floured 9″ tube pan and bake for 1 hour at 325°. After baking, let the cake stand for 10 minutes, then invert onto a rimmed plate. Prepare a sauce by combining the remaining 3/4 cup sugar with the orange and lemon juice and salt; boil gently for 3-4 minutes and pour the warm sauce over the cake.

Witch's Magic Nut Cake

Comments: Especially good at Thanksgiving or Christmas.

Preparation time: 20 minutes   Cooking time: 1 hour and 15 minutes

3 eggs
2 cups pumpkin
1/2 cup water or more
2-1/2 cups flour
2-1/4 cups sugar
1-1/2 tsp. baking soda
1-1/4 tsp. salt
3/4 cup vegetable oil

3/4 tsp. nutmeg
3/4 tsp. cinnamon
1 cup raisins
1/2 cup walnuts, chopped
4 oz. cream cheese, softened
3 tbsp. butter
1 tsp. vanilla
2 cups confectioners sugar

Beat together eggs, pumpkin, oil and water. Then add flour, sugar, soda, salt, nutmeg, cinnamon. Mix well. Add raisins and walnuts. Pour into a buttered and floured pan: 2 loaf pans or 1 Bundt pan. Bake at 350° for 1 hour, 15 minutes or until a toothpick inserted in center of the cake comes out clean. Combine the cream cheese, butter, vanilla and confectioners sugar and spread on top of the warm cake.

Berliner Kranser

YIELD: 2-3 DOZEN

Comments: A traditional German Christmas cookie.

Preparation time: 45 minutes   Cooking time: 8-10 minutes

1-1/2 hard boiled egg yolks,
  chilled
2 raw egg yolks
1/2 cup fine sugar

2 egg whites, beaten
coarsely ground lump sugar
3 cups flour
1/2 lb. butter, softened

Combine all egg yolks and blend until smooth. Beat in fine sugar. Add the butter and flour alternately until all ingredients are thoroughly blended. Roll dough into ropes approximately 1/4 to 1/2" in diameter; cut into 3" lengths and form into wreaths. Dip wreaths in the egg whites and sprinkle with the coarse sugar. Bake at 350° on buttered baking sheets until light brown, 8-10 minutes.

Lacy Oatmeal Cookies

Comments: An old-fashioned lace oatmeal cookie.

Preparation time: 10 minutes   Cooking time: 8-10 minutes

1/2 cup butter, softened	1/2 tsp. cloves
1/2 cup light brown sugar	1/2 tsp. allspice
1/4 cup sugar	1/2 tsp. ginger
1 egg	1/8 tsp. baking powder
1 cup rolled oats	1/4 cup raisins
1/4 cup flour	1/4 cup walnuts, chopped
1/2 tsp. salt	1 tsp. vanilla
1/2 tsp. cinnamon	

Cream butter and sugars. Sift dry ingredients together. Beat in egg, oats and dry ingredients. Stir in raisins, walnuts and vanilla. Drop by the teaspoonful onto a well-buttered baking sheet. Bake for 10-12 minutes at 350°.

Note: add 1/4 tsp. of all spices for a spicier cookie.

Bananas Foster

Comments: An elegant ending to a special dinner.

Preparation time: 8 minutes   Cooking time: 8 minutes

1/2 cup butter
1 cup dark brown sugar
1/8 tsp. salt
1 cup dark rum

1/2 cup Curaçao
6 large bananas, ripe but firm
1/4 cup cognac, warmed
1 quart vanilla ice cream

Melt butter in a large skillet. Add sugar and stir until dissolved. Add rum, salt and Curaçao. Heat to boiling. Slice bananas thinly and stir into syrup. Cook, stirring constantly but gently until mixture reaches the boiling point and bananas are tender. Pour the warmed cognac over the mixture and ignite. Stir until the flame is almost extinguished. Serve over ice cream.

Note: This can also be made in chafing dish at the table.

Blueberry Slump

Comments: One family's favorite for four generations!

Preparation time: 30 minutes   Cooking time: 10 minutes

3 cups blueberries, washed
  and drained
1/2 cup raspberry jam
1/2 cup water
1 tbsp. lemon juice*

*delete if berries are tart

6-8 slices white bread
butter, softened
cinnamon
light cream
1/2 cup sugar

Combine the blueberries, sugar, raspberry jam, water and lemon juice. Bring to a boil and simmer gently for 10 minutes. Remove crusts from bread, butter generously and cut into cubes. Layer half of the bread cubes in a shallow serving dish. Sprinkle lightly with cinnamon. Pour half of the fruit mixture over the bread cubes. Repeat layers. Let cool and refrigerate until serving time. Serve with light cream.

Note: Frozen berries may be substituted.

Cranberry Crunch

SERVES 6-8

Comments: A traditional New England favorite.

Preparation time: 20 minutes   Cooking time: 35 minutes

4 cups fresh cranberries,
    washed and sorted
2 tart apples, peeled, cored
    and diced
1-1/4 cups sugar
3 oz. undiluted frozen orange
    juice, thawed

1 cup flour
1/2 cup sugar
10 tbsp. butter, softened
2 tbsp. cornmeal
nutmeg
1/4 tsp. ground allspice

Combine the cranberries, apples, sugar, orange juice and allspice. Place in a shallow baking dish or 8″ square pan. Using a pastry blender, mix remaining ingredients together and spread the mixture over the cranberries. Sprinkle with nutmeg and bake at 375° for 35 minutes. If the top is not browned after baking, broil for a few minutes.

Note: Cranberries freeze well in original cello bags.

Drunk Figs

Comments: Surprisingly simple—but delicious.

Preparation time: 10 minutes   Cooking time: 45 minutes
(allow time for soaking)

1 cup dried figs	1/2 tsp. anise seed
2 cups water	1/4 cup light rum

Soak the figs in the water for 3-4 hours; cook the figs in the same water, adding the anise seed, for 45 minutes. Figs should be tender. Cool. Add 1/4 cup light rum. Chill well and serve with whipped cream, light cream, or soured cream.

Ambrosia Chiffon Pie

Comments: Light and refreshing. In tiny pie shells, delightful for tea.

Preparation time: 30 minutes

1/2 cup sugar
1/2 tsp. salt
1 tbsp. unflavoured gelatin
1 cup orange juice
3 egg yolks, lightly beaten
3 egg whites
1/2 tsp. lemon peel, shredded

1/3 cup sugar
1 cup orange sections, diced
additional orange sections
   for garnish
1/3 cup flaked coconut
9" baked pie shell
1 cup heavy cream, whipped
1 tsp. orange peel, shredded

Combine sugar, gelatin and salt in the top of a double boiler. Add the orange juice and egg yolks. Cook over hot not boiling water until the mixture is slightly thickened. Stir in the orange and lemon peels. Remove mixture to a large mixing bowl. Chill until partially set stirring occasionally. Beat the egg whites until soft peaks form; add sugar gradually and continue beating until stiff peaks form. Fold egg whites into the chilled mixture; then add the oranges and coconut. Chill again until the mixture mounds slightly when spooned. Pour into a baked pie shell and chill until set. Top with whipped cream and orange sections just before serving.

Fresh Peach Souffle

Comments: A divine seasonal dessert!

Preparation time: 1 hour and 20 minutes   Cooking time: 4-6 minutes
(allow for 8 hour refrigeration)

1 lb. ripe peaches, peeled and cut into chunks	4 eggs, separated
1 cup sugar	1/4 tsp. lemon peel, grated
1 envelope unflavoured gelatin	2 tsp. lemon juice
pinch salt	1 cup heavy cream, whipped

Mash peach chunks coarsely. Stir in 1/4 cup of the sugar and let stand for 1 hour, stirring occasionally. In the top of a double boiler combine the gelatin, 1/4 cup of sugar and pinch of salt. Drain the syrup from the peaches and add enough water to make 1/2 cup of liquid. Using a whisk thoroughly blend the egg yolks with the peach liquid. Add to the gelatin mixture and cook over simmering water for 4-6 minutes, stirring constantly. Remove from heat and add the lemon peel and juice. Place the top of the double boiler in a bowl of ice cubes, and stir the mixture until it is slightly thicker than the consistency of egg whites. Turn into large mixing bowl. Stir in peaches. Beat the egg whites, sweetened with the remaining 1/2 cup sugar, until stiff but not dry. Fold into the peach mixture. Fold in the whipped cream. Pour the mixture into a 2 quart souffle and refrigerate for 8 hours, or overnight.

Desserts   215

Brandy Pumpkin Pie

SERVES 6

Comments: A sophisticated touch for a classic New England favorite.

Prepare a pie crust and pumpkin pie filling according to your favorite recipe, substituting 1/4 cup of brandy for 1/4 cup of the liquid usually required for the filling. Bake according to recipe directions. When cool, top with whipped cream and chopped walnuts or pecans.

Glazed Cheese Pie

SERVES 6-8

Comments: A lovely summer dessert.

Preparation time: 20 minutes (allow for refrigeration).

Cooking time: 10 minutes

1 baked 9″ graham cracker
   pie shell
3/4 cup confectioners sugar
8 oz. cream cheese, softened
1 tsp. vanilla
1 cup medium cream, whipped

3 cups strawberries, fresh or
   frozen, at room temperature
1 cup sugar
3 tbsp. cornstarch
1 tbsp. lemon juice

Combine the confectioners sugar, cream cheese and vanilla and beat well. Fold in whipped cream gently. Pour into baked pie shell. Cover the strawberries with sugar and let stand for 30 minutes. Add cornstarch to the strawberry mixture. Cook until the syrup is clear and thick. Remove from heat and add the lemon juice. Pour the glaze over the top of the pie and refrigerate for several hours or overnight.

Desserts

Cloud Pie

Comments: Pleasingly light without being too sweet.

Preparation time: 2 hours   Cooking time: 1 hour
(allow for overnight refrigeration)

meringue shell	filling
3 egg whites	1 envelope unflavoured gelatin
1/4 tsp. cream of tartar	2 eggs, separated
1/4 tsp. salt	1 cup milk
3/4 cup sugar	1/3 cup cognac
1-1/2 oz. unsweetened chocolate,	1 cup heavy cream, whipped
grated	1/2 cup sugar
	1/4 tsp. salt

Meringue: beat egg whites with the cream of tartar and 1/4 tsp. of the salt until stiff but not dry. Gradually add the sugar. Beat until very stiff. Fold in the grated chocolate, reserving 1/2 tbsp. for garnish. Spread the egg white mixutre over the bottom and sides of a well-buttered 9″ pie plate. The mixture will nearly fill the pie plate. Bake at 275° for 1 hour. Chill before filling. Filling: mix the gelatin with 1/4 cup sugar and 1/4 tsp. salt in a saucepan. Beat egg yolks with milk and add to the gelatin mixture. Stir over low heat until gelatin dissolves and the mixture thickens slightly, 8-10 minutes. Remove from heat and add cognac. Chill, stirring occasionally, until the mixture mounds slightly when dropped from a spoon. Beat remaining egg whites until stiff but not dry. Gradually add the remaining 1/4 cup sugar and beat until very stiff. Fold egg whites into the gelatin mixture, then fold in the whipped cream. Spoon into the meringue shell and refrigerate overnight. Garnish with the remaining grated chocolate before serving.

Cranapple Pie

Comments: A delightful blend of fall flavours.

Preparation time: 20 minutes   Cooking time: 40-50 minutes

1-3/4 - 2 cups sugar
1/3 cup flour
crust for two-crust pie
3 cups tart apples, sliced and pared

2 cups fresh cranberries,
   washed and sorted
2 tbsp. butter
1/2 cup raisins

Mix sugar and flour together. Line a pie plate with pastry; fill with alternating layers of apples, cranberries, raisins and the sugar mixture, beginning and ending with an apple layer. Dot fruit with butter. Cover the pie with lattice-worked crust. Bake for 40-50 minutes at 425°.

Fresh Orange Pie

SERVES 8

Comments: Superb!

Preparation time: 45 minutes
(allow for refrigeration)

Cooking time: 30 minutes

4 cups orange segments
  (9 large Navel oranges)
1/2 cup sugar
1-1/2 cups orange juice
1/8 tsp. salt
dough for 1 crust pie shell

3 tbsp. corn starch
3/4 tsp. vanilla
2/3 cup apricot jam
1/2 cup toasted coconut
1 tsp. grated orange rind

To dough for 1 crust pie, add 1 tsp. grated orange rind. Line a pie plate with pastry and bake unfilled pie crust at 425° until done. Peel oranges and section into segments. Squeeze membrane and reserve juice. Pour 1/2 cup sugar over orange segments, and let stand for 1/2 hour. Drain liquid from segments add to reserved liquid making 1-1/2 cups. Add extra orange juice if necessary. Place juice in a double boiler with 1/8 tsp. salt and 3 tbsp. corn starch. Cook until the juice is thickened. Add 3/4 tsp. vanilla. Let sauce cool to room temperature. Spread 2/3 cup apricot jam on cooked pie shell. Place orange segments on top of jam. Pour cooled sauce over orange segments. Chill for at least 1 hour before serving. Garnish with toasted coconut.

Strawberry Pie

SERVES 6-8

Comments: Simple, but very special.

Preparation time: 30 minutes
(allow for refrigeration)

1 quart strawberries*	3 tbsp. cornstarch
1 cup sugar	1 cooked pie shell

may substitute blueberries, raspberries, peaches, etc.

Cover the pie shell with half of the berries reserving a few berries for garnish. Mash the remaining berries and add enough water to make 1-1/2 cups. Place mixture in saucepan and bring to a boil. Combine the sugar and cornstarch and gradually add to berry mixture. Bring to a boil a second time, stirring constantly, and boil for 1 minute. Cool, then pour into the pie shell. Chill for at least 2 hours. Before serving, top with whipped cream. Garnish with the reserved berries and sprigs of fresh mint.

Danish Coffee Pudding

Comments: Rich, with lovely texture.

Preparation time: 1 hour   Cooking time: 8-10 minutes

1 envelope unflavoured gelatin	1/2 tsp. vanilla
2 tbsp. sugar	1/2 cup cream*
1/8 tsp. salt	3 tbsp. rum
2 tbsp. instant coffee granules	1 tbsp. Kahlua, coffee brandy
1-1/4 cups milk	or Tia Maria
2 eggs, separated	1/2 cup superfine sugar

Skim milk can be substituted for the cream with excellent results.

Combine the first four ingredients in the top of a double boiler. Beat the egg yolks and milk together and add to the gelatin mixture. Let stand for 5 minutes, then cook over hot water, stirring constantly, for 8-10 minutes. Remove from heat and stir in cream and vanilla. Chill in refrigerator or over ice cubes until the mixture is cool and thick. Blend in rum and brandy. Beat egg whites until stiff; add the superfine sugar very slowly, 1 tbsp. at a time. Fold egg whites into the gelatin mixture, pour into a serving bowl or individual containers and chill thoroughly. Garnish with grated chocolate before serving.

Baked Indian Pudding

Comments: Delicious, easy and truly New England!

Preparation time: 10-15 minutes   Cooking time: 5-6 hours

6 cups hot milk	2 eggs
1 cup yellow cornmeal	1/4 tsp. salt
1/2 cup dark molasses	1/4 tsp. baking soda
1/4 cup sugar	1/4 cup butter

In a large baking dish combine 3 cups hot milk, cornmeal, molasses, sugar, butter, eggs, salt and baking soda. Blend thoroughly. Bake the mixture in a hot oven (450°) until it comes to a boil. Stir in the remaining 3 cups of milk, and transfer the mixture to a well buttered baking dish and bake for 5 to 6 hours at 250°. Serve warm, topped with vanilla ice cream or heavy cream.

Note: Bake in a crock cooker for 7-8 hours on low setting.

Easy Indian Pudding

Comments: This is an old New England specialty.

Preparation time: 5 minutes   Cooking time: 2 hours

2 tbsp. minute tapioca   1/2 cup sugar
2 tbsp. yellow cornmeal   pinch salt
1/2 cup molasses   2 tbsp. butter
1 quart whole milk

Mix all ingredients in a 2-quart casserole. Bake uncovered at 325° for 2 hours, stirring frequently. After baking, let the pudding stand at room temperature for about 2 hours, or until firm. Delicious served warm, topped with vanilla ice cream or heavy cream.

Mincemeat with Venison

Comments: While venison is nearly impossible to buy, most hunters' wives are happy to give some away! Share the work with a friend, and both will have enough for holiday gifts.

Preparation time: 2 hours   Cooking time: 2 hours
(allow for roasting meat)

4 lbs. venison roast or   3 cups molasses
   bottom round beef roast   4 cans tart cherries and juice
2 lbs. raw suet   2 lbs. seeded raisins
12 lbs. apples, pared   2 lbs. currants
2 tbsp. nutmeg   1-1/2 lbs. candied citron
2 tbsp. cinnamon   1/2 lb. candied cherries
1 tbsp. ground cloves   3 lbs. brown sugar
1 tbsp. mace   1 pint brandy
1 tbsp. salt   1 pint sherry
1 tsp. pepper   1 lb. blanched almonds
1/2 gallon cider

Roast the venison or beef until well done. Finely chop the meat, suet and apples. Mix with all spices; add molasses, cherries and juice from the cherries. Bring to a boil and add the currants, raisins, citron, candied cherries and brown sugar. Cook for 2 hours, then add brandy, sherry and blanched almonds. Place in sterilized jars and seal. Store in a cool dry place.

Note: One jar will make one 8" pie.

Nanna's Mincemeat Pudding

Comments: A holiday tradition for generations. Makes a wonderful gift.

Preparation time: 30 minutes   Cooking time: 3 hours

2 cups mincemeat	1 egg
1 tsp. baking soda	2 cups flour
1/2 tsp. salt	1 tsp. baking powder
2 tbsp. butter, melted	

Add the soda to the mincemeat. It will foam. Blend in egg, then butter, then dry ingredients, mixing well after each addition. Pour into a well-buttered mold. Place mold in a baking pan with 1" hot water and steam for 3 hours. Add more water if necessary while the pudding is cooking. Let cool for 15 minutes in the mold, then remove. Serve with Foamy Sauce.

Foamy Sauce

Comments: Serve over mincemeat pudding or other steamed pudding.

Preparation time: 5 minutes

1 cup whipping cream	2 tsp. vanilla
1 egg	1 cup confectioners sugar
4 tbsp. butter, melted	

Whip cream until stiff. Beat egg; add sugar, vanilla and butter. Fold whipped cream into egg mixture. Refrigerate until serving time.

Charlotte Russe

SERVES 8

Comments: Light and delicate in texture.

Preparation time: 20-30 minutes   Cooking time: 5 minutes
(allow for refrigeration)

1-1/2 dozen lady fingers	6 egg yolks
2 envelopes unflavoured gelatin	1/4 cup bourbon or 2 tsp. vanilla
1/2 cup cold water	2 cups whipping cream
2 cups milk	1 cup sugar

Line a charlotte mold with lady fingers. Soften the gelatin in cold water. Scald the milk. Beat egg yolks and sugar until the mixture forms "ribbons" when the beater is lifted from the bowl. Stir in the scalded milk. Cook in a large saucepan until the mixture begins to thicken. Add gelatin and stir until it is dissolved. Add the bourbon or vanilla and set aside to cool. Whip cream and fold into the egg mixture. Pour into the charlotte mold and chill until firm. Unmold on a cake stand.

Note: Any 2-qt mold may be substituted; cut lady fingers to size.

Creamy Chocolate Celeste

SERVES 8

Comments: Divinely chocolate!

Preparation time: 20 minutes   Cooking time: 5 minutes
(allow for refrigeration)

8 oz. chocolate chips   2 eggs, separated
1 oz. unsweetened chocolate   1 tbsp. brandy
2 tbsp. butter   2 cups whipping cream
2 tbsp. strong coffee   grated chocolate
pinch salt   walnuts, finely chopped

Melt chocolate with butter over hot, not boiling water, stirring to blend until smooth. Remove from heat and add the coffee, salt, egg yolks, and brandy. Cool for 5 minutes. Beat egg whites until stiff and fold into the chocolate mixture. Whip cream until it mounds but is not too stiff. Fold in gently until a marbled effect is achieved. Spoon into dessert dishes, mounding high. Chill for several hours or overnight. Before serving top with a small amount of whipped cream and garnish with shaved unsweetened chocolate or finely chopped walnuts.

Mocha Pots de Creme

SERVES 4

Comments: A short-cut to an elegant finale.

Preparation time: 5 minutes

1 cup heavy cream	1 tsp. unsweetened cocoa
1-1/2 tsp. instant coffee granules	1/2 cup confectioners sugar

Combine all ingredients and whip until thick. Pour into pots de creme or demi-tasses and chill.

U.S. Frigate Constitution, of 44 Guns
by William Lynn and Abel Bowen, circa 1813
Courtesy of the Museum of Fine Arts, Boston, Massachusetts

Bisque Ice Cream

Comments: Our version of Tortoni!

Preparation time: 15 minutes
(allow 24 hours for dehydrating macaroons)

1 cup macaroon crumbs	2 tbsp. sugar
1 egg yolk	1 cup cream, whipped
2 tbsp. rum	

Allow crumbled macaroons to dry out for about 24 hours. Blend the crumbs with the egg yolk. Add the rum and sugar. Fold in the whipped cream. Rinse a small mold in cold water and pour the mixture into the wet mold and freeze.

Mocha Mousse

Comments Very rich, very chocolatey!

Preparation time: 20 minutes
(allow for refrigeration)

3 oz. unsweetened chocolate	1 tbsp. instant coffee granules
1/3 cup water	1/2 tsp. vanilla
3/4 cup sugar	1 cup heavy cream
3 egg yolks	

Combine chocolate and water in a heavy saucepan and heat slowly, stirring constantly. When chocolate is melted, add sugar and coffee granules and cook over a low heat for 2 minutes, stirring constantly. Beat egg yolks in a bowl until they are lemon-coloured. Add the chocolate mixture to the eggs beating constantly. Whip the cream, add vanilla, and fold into the cooled chocolate mixture. Pour into a 1 quart mold. Refrigerate for at least 4 hours.

Pots de Creme

Comments: An exceptional "basic" recipe with interesting variations.

Preparation time: 10 minutes)
(allow for refrigeration)

1 cup semi-sweet chocolate bits	1 cup heavy cream, whipped
1 egg	grated unsweetened chocolate
3 tbsp. instant coffee granules	3/4 cup medium cream or milk,
2 tbsp. rum	scalded
	pinch salt

Place chocolate bits, sugar, egg, liquor and salt in blender. Add hot cream. Blend until smooth. Pour into pots de creme and chill several hours or overnight. Garnish with whipped cream just before serving.

Note: a.) substitute Grand Marnier for the rum
      b.) substitute chocolate mint chips for plain chocolate chips and for a very minty flavour substitute creme de menthe for the rum.

White Velvet

Comments: Simple ingredients, sophisticated results! Especially good in the summer when fresh fruits are plentiful.

Preparation time: 10 minutes)
(allow for refrigeration)

2 cups heavy cream	2 tbsp. cold water
1/2 cup sugar	1 pint soured cream
1 tbsp. unflavoured gelatin	pinch salt
	fresh fruit

Heat the cream, stirring constantly, just to the boiling point. Remove from heat. Add sugar and salt. Soften gelatin in water and add to the hot cream. Stir until the gelatin is dissolved, then blend in the soured cream. Pour the mixture into a ring mold and chill until firm. Before serving, unmold onto a chilled platter and fill the center with fruit.

Zabaglione Mousse

Comments: A pleasant variation of a European favorite.

Preparation time: 20 minutes   Cooking time: 5 minutes
(allow for refrigeration)

6 egg yolks, well beaten	1 cup heavy cream
1/2 cup sugar	1/3 cup Grand Marnier or
1 envelope unflavoured gelatin	any orange flavoured liqueur

Blend egg yolks and sugar together. In a separate bowl, whip cream lightly and reserve. Combine the gelatin and Grand Marnier in a small saucepan. Heat slowly until dissolved. Combine the egg and sugar mixture and the cream. Then add the gelatin. Beat in a mixing bowl which is surrounded by cracked ice until the mixture thickens. Add more Grand Marnier to taste: 1-2 tbsp. Pour into a lightly oiled 1 quart mold and chill until firm.

Cheese Bees' Knees

YIELD: 5 DOZEN

Comments: Attractive and tasty morsels to serve with tea.

Preparation time: 30 minutes   Cooking time: 30 minutes

24 oz. cream cheese, softened
1-1/2 cups sugar
5 eggs
1-1/2 tsp. vanilla

1 can cherry pie filling
1 cup soured cream
petite muffin pans or
   small cupcake liners

Cream cheese with 1 cup of the sugar. Add eggs, one at a time. Add vanilla. Pour batter into small paper cups and place them in petite muffin pans. Bake at 350° for 25 minutes. Mix the soured cream with the remaining 1/2 cup sugar. Spoon a small amount of this mixture over the top of each of the "cakes" and bake for an additional 5 minutes. Cool, then top each with one cherry from the can of pie filling. Serve at room temperature.

Golden Bars

Comments: An interesting caramel flavour.

Preparation time: 15 minutes   Cooking time: 30-35 minutes

2/3 cup butter	3 eggs, well beaten
1-1/2 cups flour	1/4 tsp. salt
2 cups brown sugar	1 tsp. vanilla
2 tsp. baking powder	3/4 cup walnuts, chopped

Melt butter in a saucepan; remove from heat. Sift flour, baking powder and salt. Stir in remaining ingredients. Mix thoroughly. Spread batter in a buttered and floured 9" x 13" pan. Bake at 325° for 30-35 minutes. Cool before cutting into squares.

Thin Chocolate Squares

Comments: Delicious with dessert or demitasse!

Preparation time: 30 minutes   Cooking time: 10-12 minutes

1/2 cup butter, softened	1/2 cup flour
2-1/2 squares unsweetened	1 tsp. vanilla
chocolate, melted	powdered sugar
2 eggs, beaten	1 cup walnuts or pecans, chopped
1 cup brown sugar	

Cream butter and sugar. Add the beaten eggs, chocolate, flour, nuts and vanilla. Spread the batter evenly on a buttered and floured baking sheet. Bake at 325° for 10-12 minutes. Sprinkle the top with powdered sugar while still warm and cut into squares.

Lemon Loves

Comments: Divine!

Preparation time: 5-10 minutes   Cooking time: 45 minutes

1 cup butter	4 tbsp. flour
2 cups flour	1 tsp. baking powder
1/2 cup powdered sugar	6 tbsp. lemon juice
4 eggs	rind of 1 lemon, grated
2 cups sugar	pinch salt

Blend butter, flour and powdered sugar together thoroughly. Press to line a well buttered and floured 9" x 13" pan. Bake at 350° for 25 minutes. Watch closely. Beat eggs until frothy. Add all remaining ingredients and beat until smooth. Pour into the crust and bake for 20-25 minutes at 350°. Dust with powdered sugar. Refrigerate until serving time. Cut into squares.

Note: This recipe can be made as a pie. Adjust quantity for different size pan.

Meringue Champignons

Comments: An elegant sweet to serve with tea or give to a special friend!

Preparation time: 20 minutes   Cooking time: 30-40 minutes

1 egg white	1/4 cup sugar
dash cream of tartar	semi-sweet chocolate

Butter and flour a cookie sheet. Beat the egg white until foamy; add sugar and continue beating until stiff peaks form. Spoon the mixture into a pastry bag with a large round tip. Don't fill it too full. Hold bag close to the cookie sheet and press out 3/4″ wide "caps". Smooth out peak on top if any. Form the stems separately by holding the bag vertically and pressing out a small quantity. Each of the "stems" should look like chocolate kisses with a point on top. Bake until dry and ivory-coloured 30 to 40 minutes. Loosen with spatula and cool on a wire rack. Make a small hole in the underside of each cap while still warm and insert stem piece. The underside of each mushroom can be brushed with melted semi-sweet chocolate.

Spiced Pecans

Comments: So delicious they could be habit-forming! Terrific for the holidays or as a hostess gift.

Preparation time: 5 minutes   Cooking time: 30 minutes

1 egg white	1/2 tsp. salt
2 tbsp. water	1 tsp. cinnamon
2 cups pecans	1/4 tsp. ground cloves
1/2 cup sugar	1/4 tsp. nutmeg

Beat egg white and water; mix in pecans. In a separate bowl combine the sugar, salt and spices. Sprinkle over the nuts and mix thoroughly. Spread the nuts on a buttered baking sheet. Bake for 30 minutes at 300°. Cool on waxed paper.

Rum Yums

YIELD: 5 DOZEN

Comments: A lovely Christmas cookie!

Preparation time: 10 minutes   Cooking time: 10 minutes

1 cup brown sugar	1/2 cup rum
1/2 cup butter	1-1/2 tsp. baking soda dissolved
2 cups flour, sifted	in 1 tbsp. milk
2 eggs	1/4 lb. citron
1/2 tsp. nutmeg	1 lb. walnuts
1/2 tsp. cloves	1 lb. raisins

Cream butter and sugar. Blend in remaining ingredients, mixing until citron, walnuts and raisins are evenly distributed through dough. Work dough with hands if it is too stiff. Drop by 1/2 teaspoonful onto baking sheet. Bake at 350° for 10 minutes.

English Butter Toffee

Comments: Real candy-store quality.

Preparation time: 10 minutes   Cooking time: 30 minutes

3/4 lb. butter	5 oz. milk chocolate, melted
2 cups sugar	3 oz. toasted almonds, chopped

Cook butter and sugar slowly in a deep heavy saucepan to the hard crack stage (300-310°). Pour into a large buttered pan and cool. Brush the top with melted chocolate and sprinkle with chopped almonds. Cool until the chocolate has set. Lift and invert the toffee on a piece of waxed paper. Brush the other side with melted chocolate and sprinkle with almonds. Break into pieces.

Trilly Bars

YIELD: 2-1/2 DOZEN BARS

Comments: Delicious on a Sunday afternoon sitting by the fire!

Preparation time: 30 minutes   Cooking time: 30 minutes

1-1/2 cups flour	3/4 cup butter, softened
1-3/4 cups quick-cooking oatmeal	1 cup dates, finely chopped
2 cups brown sugar	1 cup water
1/2 tsp. salt	1 tsp. baking powder

Combine the dates, water and 1 cup of the brown sugar in a saucepan, and cook until thick enough to spread. Cool. Sift flour, salt and baking powder. Add the oatmeal and remaining brown sugar and mix until the ingredients are thoroughly blended. Cut the butter into the dough and work until the dough is moist and crumbly. Press half of the mixture into the bottom of a 9″ x 11″ baking pan. Spread the date mixture evenly over the dough; sprinkle the remaining dough over the dates and pat firmly into place. Bake at 350° for 30 minutes. Cool in the baking pan and cut into squares.

Potpourri

Chutney

Comments: A great recipe and a delightful gift!

Preparation time: 45 minutes   Cooking time: 2 hours

3-1/2 lbs. pears, peaches or
   mangoes, firm, not soft
2 large cloves garlic, minced
3-1/2 cups sugar
4 tbsp. Worcestershire sauce
1-1/2 cups vinegar
1/2 tsp. ground ginger

1 tbsp. whole mustard seed
1 cup onions, chopped
3/4 cup lime juice
1/2 tsp. crushed red pepper
1/2 cup seedless raisins
1/2 cup golden raisins
2 oz. crystalized ginger,
   finely slivered

Peel, core and slice fruit 1/4″ thick. Mix the sugar, vinegar, Worcestershire sauce, ground ginger and garlic. Bring the syrup to a boil and add the fruit. Cook slowly until the fruit is clear. Add the remaining ingredients and cook until the onion is tender and the mixture is thick. Pack in hot sterilized jars and seal. Tighten covers when jars are cool enough to handle. Store in a cool place.

Cranberry Chutney

Comments: Piquant.

Preparation time: 10 minutes   Cooking time: 30-40 minutes

1 cup water
4 cups fresh cranberries,
   washed and sorted
1 cup raisins
1 small can pineapple,
   chopped and drained

1/2 tsp. ginger
1/2 tsp. cinnamon
1/4 tsp. allspice
1/4 tsp. salt
2 cups sugar

Combine water, cranberries, raisins, sugar, spices and salt in a large saucepan. Mix well and cook over medium heat until the cranberries pop and the mixture begins to thicken; about 20 minutes. Stir in the drained pineapple. Continue cooking for an additional 20 minutes or until the sauce has reached the desired consistency. Cool and store in the refrigerator for up to two weeks.

Cranberry Fruit Conserve

Comments: A seasonal specialty — rich, but delicate.

Preparation time: 15 minutes   Cooking time: 20 minutes

4 cups fresh cranberries, washed and sorted
1-1/2 cups water
2-1/2 cups sugar
1 cup seeded raisins

1 cup walnuts
grated rind and juice of 1 orange
grated rind and juice of 1 lemon
1 apple, peeled, cored and coarsely chopped

Cook cranberries in water until all the skins pop open. Add the sugar, raisins, apple, orange juice and rind, lemon juice and rind; cook for 15 minutes. Remove from heat and add walnuts. Chill before serving.

Almond Cranberry Sauce

Comments: Elegant and festive! A delightful change from the usual cranberry sauce.

Preparation time: 20 minutes   Cooking time: 15 minutes

**4 cups fresh cranberries,
   washed and sorted
1/2 cup apricot jam or
   preserves**

**1 cup water
1/2 cup toasted almond slivers
1/4 cup lemon juice
2 cups sugar**

Combine sugar and water in a large saucepan. Bring to a boil and cook for 5 minutes over medium heat. Add the cranberries and cook for an additional 3-5 minutes, or until the cranberries pop open. Remove the pan from the heat and stir in the jam and lemon juice. Chill; add almonds.

Port Wine Cranberry Sauce

YIELD: 3 CUPS

Comments: A delightfully elegant change from the usual cranberry sauce.

Preparation time: 5 minutes   Cooking time: 5 minutes

2-3 cups fresh cranberries,   1/2 cup sugar
    washed and sorted   1-2 tbsp. butter
2/3 cup water   3 tbsp. Port wine

Simmer the cranberries in the water and sugar until they pop. Add the butter. Add the Port and cool thoroughly before serving.

A Prospect of the Colleges in Cambridge in New England
by William Burgis, 1726
Courtesy of the Massachusetts Historical Society, Boston, Massachusetts

Hot Curried Fruit

SERVES 8

Comments: A fruit melange which knows no season.

Preparation time: 20 minutes
(allow for overnight refrigeration)

Cooking time: 1 hour

1 can pears
1 can peaches
1 can apricots
1 can red sour pie cherries
1 can chunk pineapple

1/2 cup butter
3/4 cup brown sugar
1-1/2 tsp. curry powder
3 tbsp. cornstarch

Drain fruit well and arrange in a baking dish. Melt butter; add sugar, curry powder and cornstarch. The mixture will be very thick. Spoon the sauce over the fruit; cover and refrigerate for 24 hours. Uncover and bake at 350° for 1 hour. Serve hot.

Winter Compote

Comments: A lovely tart condiment when citrus and winter pears are available.

Preparation time: 10 minutes   Cooking time: 1 hour

1 cup light corn syrup
1 orange, peeled and sectioned
1 cup fresh cranberries, washed
  and sorted

6 whole cloves
3″ stick cinnamon
3 fresh pears, peeled, cored
  and quartered

Place all ingredients in an oven-proof dish; cover and bake at 350° for 1 hour or until the pears are tender. Chill thoroughly before serving.

Note: Add more fruit for a thicker consistency.

Tomato Juice

Comments: Try this in late summer when tomatoes are plentiful.

Preparation time: 30 minutes   Cooking time: 2 hours

4-5 lbs. ripe tomatoes, pref. Beefsteak
1 green pepper
1/2 bunch celery, including leaves
several sprigs fresh basil
2 cups water

1 large onion, chopped
5-6 peppercorns
1/4 cup salt
1 carrot, chopped
sugar to taste
1/2 cup fresh parsley

Wash and cut tomatoes, removing any questionable soft areas. Put in a large kettle with all remaining ingredients, except sugar. Bring to a boil. Reduce heat and simmer until all vegetables are very soft, stirring occasionally. Put through a food mill or sieve. Return to heat and add sugar to taste and any other seasonings of your own choice. Bring the juice to a boil. Pour into sterilized jars and seal.

Note: This juice is thick. Can be served as juice, used in tomato aspic, or served as soup. Thin with beef bouillon and add a dash of sherry for a special brunch soup.

Granny's Tomato Relish

YIELD: 8-10 PINTS

Comments: Take this to your weekend hostess on the Vineyard!

Preparation time: 35 minutes   Cooking time: about 3 hours

24 ripe tomatoes, peeled	1-1/2 cups brown sugar
12 medium onions	2 cups vinegar
3 green peppers	1 tbsp. cinnamon
3 tbsp. salt	1 tbsp. ground cloves
2 tbsp. crushed red pepper	1 tbsp. mustard

Chop vegetables and combine with other ingredients. Bring to a slow boil and simmer until mushy and the juice has thickened. Stir occasionally to prevent scorching. Pack in hot sterile jars. Screw lids down very tightly. Tighten covers again when jars have reached handling temperature.

Index

PRESENTING BOSTON
The Junior League of Boston, Inc.
117 Newbury Street
Boston, Massachusetts 02116

Please send me _____ copies of your cookbook at $10.95 per copy plus
$1.50 for postage and handling. Enclosed is my check or money order made
out to PRESENTING BOSTON for $ _____.

Name _____

Street _____

City _____ State _____ Zip _____

Massachusetts residents please include 5% sales tax

. . . .

PRESENTING BOSTON
The Junior League of Boston, Inc.
117 Newbury Street
Boston, Massachusetts 02116

Please send me _____ copies of your cookbook at $10.95 per copy plus
$1.50 for postage and handling. Enclosed is my check or money order made
out to PRESENTING BOSTON for $ _____.

Name _____

Street _____

City _____ State _____ Zip _____

Massachusetts residents please include 5% sales tax

. . . .

PRESENTING BOSTON
The Junior League of Boston, Inc.
117 Newbury Street
Boston, Massachusetts 02116

Please send me _____ copies of your cookbook at $10.95 per copy plus
$1.50 for postage and handling. Enclosed is my check or money order made
out to PRESENTING BOSTON for $ _____.

Name _____

Street _____

City _____ State _____ Zip _____

Massachusetts residents please include 5% sales tax